The First Time We Met The Blues

THE FIRST TIME WE MET THE BLUES

A journey of discovery with Jimmy Page, Brian Jones, Mick Jagger and Keith Richards

David Williams

MUSIC MENTOR BOOKS

York, England

British Library Cataloguing-in-Publication Data
A catalogue record for this book is available from the British Library.

ISBN-13: 978-0-9547068-1-4

Published worldwide by Music Mentor Books *(Proprietor: G.R. Groom-White)*
69 Station Rd, Upper Poppleton, York YO26 6PZ, North Yorks, England.
Telephone: +44 (0)1904 330308 *Email:* music.mentor@lineone.net

Cover by It's Great To Be Rich, York.

Printed and bound in Great Britain by Bonacia Ltd, Peterborough.

For Anna, Gareth and Kieron

Front cover

Photos of (top to bottom) John Lee Hooker,
T-Bone Walker and Willie Dixon by Brian Smith.

Photo of Manchester Free Trade Hall by Chris Cooney.
Special thanks to Angela Smith.

FOREWORD
BY JIMMY PAGE

Today, nearly everyone would know that rock music came into being via the blues. However, back when I was still a teenager, exposure to such music in Britain was almost non-existent and the recordings available to us were few and far between and very hard to find. While growing up in Epsom I gradually expanded my record collection, and by 1962 I had developed a real appreciation of artists such as Muddy Waters and Howlin' Wolf.

When David told me of the impending visit of the initial *American Folk-Blues Festival* to England I was keen to join the pilgrimage to Manchester. It was not only the first time that I would actually see artists like John Lee Hooker and T-Bone Walker perform, but it was also the first time I met Mick Jagger, Brian Jones and Keith Richards, who came with us on the trip. We were all like-minded enthusiasts and in those days we regarded the artists we were going to see as idols.

Hopefully this book will tell the story of our youthful enthusiasm for the blues and provide the reader with an idea of what a voyage of discovery it was for us.

Jimmy Page
London, March 2009

CONTENTS

INTRODUCTION & ACKNOWLEDGEMENTS

Let's get one thing straight right from the start. All of you considering reading further will almost certainly know more about the careers of the Rolling Stones and Led Zeppelin than I do. However, if you do continue turning the pages, you will discover a few things about some of the individuals in those groups that you have never read about anywhere else. That said, this book is as much about me, Graham Ackers and the others as it is about Jimmy Page, Mick Jagger, Keith Richards and Brian Jones, for on our voyage of discovery we were all in it together.

Although there is quite a bit of scene-setting, the central focus of this book is our trip to the first ever *American Folk-Blues Festival*, which visited Britain for just a single night in 1962. Just how important a musical influence that concert and the events that led up to it was on the people who attended I must leave for others to judge, for I don't feel qualified to comment on their eventual successes. At the time, it seemed like a life-or-death quest to rival the search for the Holy Grail. Looking back now, it was all never anything less than fun.

Some concentrated effort has been needed, for little of what has recently come to mind had ever really occupied my thoughts until now. Certainly, a few after-dinner tales and 'down the pub' stories have taken place over the years, but that was about the extent of my recollections. I am sure it would have remained that way had it not been for the recent interest in the *American Folk-Blues* tours of the Sixties and the celebration of the 40th anniversary of those concerts. Some friends and colleagues felt that there were readers who would be interested in those far-off days and I toyed with the task for while.

Then, out of the blue, I received a phone call from the award-winning American author, Rob Bowman. He informed me that some old black & white German television film of the early tours had been discovered and was about to become the subject of several DVDs on Hip-O. My long-time friend, John Broven, had told him of our little expedition to see the very first of them. So, Rob briefly interviewed me for the booklet that accompanied their release and, considering the new interest, I was encouraged to progress.

I feel I must emphasise that at no time was this intended to be a scrupulously researched study with meticulous cross-references to other learned works on every page. I have read a few of those sorts of books and have found that the notes, quotes, index and 'ographies' etc often seem to occupy almost as many pages as the text. To be frank, I have not really read much in the in the way of written works about Zeppelin or the Stones anyway. My ignorance would possibly be mourned by all but myself, but at least what you are getting here is just what I remember and not a mechanical journalistic reworking of someone else's experiences.

I am aware that some readers will thirst for minute detail. But, I have to say that Eskimo tailoring is not really to my taste, so those still partial to wearing anoraks will remain frustrated, for I am unable to supply anyone's dental records or National Insurance numbers. Likewise, those desperately in search of juicy gossip and scandal had better continue reading the tabloid press, for this is intended to be an affectionate recollection of a youthful period of musical discovery which happens to involve individuals who have since become world famous, and nothing more.

I left Britain shortly after the events recorded here and spent the next few years working my way around the world. By the time I returned, the Rolling Stones and Led Zeppelin were both household names and I had lost touch with the guys. Perhaps I felt intimidated by their celebrity status and renewed contact seemed inappropriate. In retrospect, this is regrettable, for Jim in particular was a very good friend to me in my youth. But one cannot turn back the clock. My passion for black rhythm & blues turned out to be a lifelong monogamous love affair that more or less precluded other forms of music and, anyway, their subsequent careers are extensively documented elsewhere. But, if you want to know what happened before the great flood, I will do my best to tell you for, in the words of Welsh rugby folklore, 'I know because I was there'.

More than forty years have elapsed since the events recorded here took place, so readers will have to forgive me if these recollections are sometimes a little incomplete or vague. I trust they are as correct as I can make them. You will hopefully appreciate that some seriously worn and grey brain cells were put to the test, and I sincerely thank all who have prompted and helped me along the way. I am not going to name them all but a few must be mentioned.

Graham Ackers who hired and drove the van that took us all to

Manchester remains a dear friend, but his powers of recall seem to need more fuelling with alcohol as the years go by! We did consider trying to hypnotise him but I'm not sure that would work, and anyway, I fear some of the results might be unprintable! Dave Ward, whose flat we invaded, was very helpful, as was Will Jones, Dickie Tapp, Dave Clark, Bill Bailey, Mark Howson, Brian Smith, John 'Jumbo' Spicer, Bill Moodie and Cilla Huggins, the editor of *Juke Blues* magazine. I must not forget my amazing wife, Anna. She was there, too, when most of this took place and, as with many other things in my life, I could not have done this without her. If I have missed anyone out, I apologise. Thank you all anyway.

Why did I call the book *The First Time We Met The Blues*? Well, for us it *was* the first time any of us encountered this sort of music in the flesh. No buts, maybes or last times, this was the *first* time.

Coincidentally, at about the same time these events took place, Buddy Guy was just about ready to forge his reputation in Europe aided by a song called 'The First Time I Met The Blues'. In a way, he could have been singing it for us.

Although we were unaware at the time, we were not the first Brits to see real American blues artists: a previous generation of traditional (ie Dixieland) jazz enthusiasts had been treated to occasional visits, mainly due to the efforts of British bandleader Chris Barber. Big Bill Broonzy and Brother John Sellers toured with the Barber band in the mid-Fifties. At that time, many regarded the blues as a subdivision of jazz, while others felt it was acoustic folk music. In a way, both factions were correct, yet somehow Britain was not really ready to accept the blues in the way that it is now regarded worldwide.

The arrival of Muddy Waters with his Fender electric guitar and his pianist Otis Spann in 1958 certainly caused controversy among the bearded corduroy brigade. Many regarded the amplification as noisy and vulgar but he, and the visionary Barber, were probably just ahead of their time. Ironically, when Muddy returned to Britain with the 1963 *American Folk-Blues Festival* tour, he used an acoustic guitar, which, during the ensuing period had suddenly become passé and many in the audience were sorely disappointed.

We only became aware of these visits in retrospect, and even if we had known of them at the time, we would have been too young to attend. Besides, our initial interest in the blues came from an altogether different direction.

So, once upon a time, a long, long time ago…

PART ONE

JIMMY AND ROCK'N'ROLL

I

Jim and I grew up in Epsom, which, in those days, was a market town approximately twenty-five miles south of Central London. Then it had the feel of a relatively small English country town, while now it seems to be a connected part of the capital's urban sprawl and is probably the very definition of suburbia. The centre is divided by the main street running roughly north to south, and the affluent area, where the majority of the city commuters lived, was to the east up towards those famous Downs where horse racing and the Derby took place. We lived on the other side of the divide in a crescent-shaped little street called Miles Road. Jim's house at number 34 was nearer the town end and backed on to the railway line to London; mine at number 122 was at the other and had the local sewage farm for a vista. It was not a plush place to live, that's for sure, but pleasant enough as long as the wind blew in the right direction.

As if to reinforce my view of the town, a friend recently brought to my attention the release of a retrospective double CD of early Eric Clapton recordings, that is modestly entitled *Clapton Is God – The Cream of Early Eric*. Included are four tracks that are early collaborations with Jimmy. One of those cuts is actually entitled 'Miles Road', so I guess Jim had an affection for our little old street as well.

When I use the phrase 'grew up', I suppose I mean from short trousers and bloody knees onwards, for I cannot remember Jim before the age of about eight or nine. There were plenty of wartime babies sprouting in our road and we did all the usual things that kids of that age do. I can remember us having roller skates, fights in the bridge alley, and street football with old tennis balls and goals chalked on the road kerbs. The latter was a safe enough pursuit as hardly anyone in the road owned a car and we were never in any real peril from the milkman's electric cart.

Although we lived in the same street, for some reason we did not go to the same school. I think Jim's dad worked for a plastic-coating company in Chessington, while mine worked at the local hospital. Our fathers had a nodding acquaintance with each other at the bus stop on the main road, but that was about the extent of their familiarity.

I was once told that some sadly mistaken journalist had suggested that Page Motors, the garage and car sales showroom in the High Street, was Jim's parents' family business. I had to laugh, for if that had been the case, he would surely not have been living in Miles Road and would probably have had his so-desired Fender at a much earlier age. My grandmother and aunt lived almost opposite his house, and I now suspect that is how Jim and I first met.

As much of what you read here is to be devoted to music matters, it is probably useful at this point to give you a brief idea of the British musical climate in the early Fifties.

II

I was about a year older than Jim, and by 1954 we were both approaching our teens. This was at the tail-end of a long period of post-war austerity in Britain. At this time, young people in Britain had almost no disposable income and little influence, if any, over the sort of music they could listen to. Few parents possessed record players and, if they did, their tastes were governed by the music they could hear on the radio. The British Broadcasting Corporation was almost the only English language broadcasting medium readily available and, as far as we were concerned, the crusty old Establishment ruled. It seemed that *Two-Way Family Favourites* and *Housewives' Choice* were the only programmes where popular music of the day could be heard and, to our eager young ears, it didn't make very radical or inspiring listening. The eventual fifty-year copyright expiry and the subsequent cashing-in by CD reissue companies did, of course, reveal that there was some very interesting alternative music around at the time, but it was not readily available to us in Britain.

On our airwaves big band swing, crooners and novelty songs were the order of the day. Frank Sinatra, Dean Martin and Perry Como were the hot acts. How about that Perry C, what a funky dude was he! I am sure that the young George Bush must have had him as an early role model, for they both seem to have been to the same tailor, hairdresser and posture coach. It's all a matter of taste, of course, for forty years later these dinosaurs became the trendy fashion again and my last place of work was at an office above a Pizza Express restaurant where they played their old hits every afternoon. The sound of their music came wafting up with the smell of sizzling pepperoni and I guess that was what finally broke this camel's back and convinced me to give up the job and do something different.

Despite the dominance of the BBC, down at the bottom end of the radio dial at 208 on the Medium Wave band lurked the independent and commercially financed Radio Luxembourg, with its poor reception and the merest hint of what lay in wait around the corner. I celebrated my first teenage birthday in 1955 and, in retrospect, the advent and discovery of rock'n'roll was my much-needed present, for it was around this time that my mother died unexpectedly.

My caring father clearly felt I needed a little extra slack and allowed me to have an old valve radio in my bedroom. It was an enormous mahogany box with speaker cover on the front and a dimly lit dial on the top. I became a regular Luxembourg listener, and occasionally there was the hint of something a little stronger than the regular Top Ten fare. However, one night I played with the tuning knob and accidentally found the American Forces Network. American accents were in themselves highly attractive to an impressionable young lad, but my interest escalated sharply when one night I encountered a fifteen-minute programme presented by rock'n'roll disc jockey Alan Freed. The reception was very poor and you would probably only get to hear five or six numbers per show. Nevertheless, one song he played was the utterly spellbinding 'Too Much Monkey Business' by someone whose name I thought sounded a bit like Chuck 'Crazy Legs' Perry. I did not know what the hell he was singing about, but I thought it all sounded quite fantastic.

I soon learnt that a boy in my class at school had a sister who worked at the nearby Decca record factory and that she could get records to order at discount prices. It was via this route that I obtained an extended play disc by the man with the strange name. It was, of course, Chuck Berry.

My father was a very tolerant parent, and I guess he spoilt me a bit. As far as I can recall, he had little or no interest in popular music of the day, but it was he who bought me my first record player shortly after the death of my mother. Actually, it was more a piece of furniture than a functional machine for playing records. I think it gloried in the grand

Jim's house at 34 Miles Road.

title of a 'radiogram' and it stood in the corner of our front room like a polished mahogany desk. Never mind what it looked like, it had a bloody good speaker that would be thoroughly tested to destruction in the coming years.

Peter Neal (who lived at the very end of the street nearest Jim's house), Jim and I were inseparable friends at this time in our lives. Like Jim, I was an only child and, with no brothers and sisters to get in the way, we would often hang out at his or my house for as long as our parents could tolerate. All three of us were intensely interested in this new music and we played that Chuck Berry record until the grooves started to look white. 'Maybellene' and 'Thirty Days' were the songs that had the rhythm and excitement that stimulated Jimmy, but the slow, bluesy 'Wee Wee Hours' with its evocative piano solo was the track that really impressed me.

I think I can just about remember Jim getting his first guitar and having some initial lessons. But, try as I may, I cannot recall how he became involved with a local skiffle group. It may have been through his school friends and, although it was a relatively brief episode, I do know that they achieved a level of local fame by making an appearance on a BBC children's television programme. However, I do know that a boy named David Housego was involved. He lived in the house with the largest plot of land at the apex of our crescent. His father actually had a car, which was a real sign of affluence, but even more impressive was his dad's drum kit. The man had apparently dabbled with the drums in a dance band at some time in the past, and David was attempting to follow in his father's footsteps. I did not know him particularly well, and the family soon moved to more upmarket surroundings of nearby Ashtead and we lost touch.

I am certain that Jim's mother was the initial driving force behind his musical progression. She was a petite, dark-haired woman with a strong personality, a glint in her eye and wicked sense of humour. She liked to tease me in a good-natured way, but let me hang out endlessly in their front room with Jim. I think she must have known my mother and, given the new circumstances I found myself in, I guess she felt sorry for me. Although I didn't realise it at the time, I can now appreciate her kindness and tolerance, for I must have been a fairly constant presence in her house.

Our houses were tiny, semi-detached buildings with two living rooms on the ground floor bisected by a central staircase to two bedrooms above. Access was by the main entrance door at the side of the house. There was an attached kitchen at the back and an outside toilet, which most people eventually replaced with a bathroom extension that you reached by avoiding whatever was cooking on the stove. Very hygienic, I'm sure.

That small front room at Jim's house became the centre of our world. Jim must have had equally tolerant neighbours, for we did make a racket in that tiny space. Peter had brothers and sisters to escape from, and most of the time I had an empty house to leave behind. We started to buy the *Melody Maker* (a tabloid newspaper-styled publication devoted to jazz and popular music) and soon found that there were a few more interesting examples of the new music available than those which made the hit parade and the radio. We quickly learnt to 'read between the lines' and interpret names, titles and record labels in order to discover the exotic goodies we now so passionately desired.

Decca was one of the few major British record companies, and they had a subsidiary named London American which leased successful recordings from small emerging US independent companies like Chess, Atlantic, Specialty, etc, and their names would be included in the small print on the label. As far as we were concerned, these were important indicators and invariably a passport to exciting listening. However, we had very little money to spend and such records were carefully chosen precious items.

Jim was always way ahead of us in technological matters and he was the first amongst us to acquire a reel-to-reel tape recorder. When he eventually moved on to a bigger and better model, I inherited the old one from him, and we then had the means to tape and share music. This would prove immensely useful in the coming years and enabled us to expand our knowledge on a limited budget.

Initially our tastes were mainly focused on the likes of Jerry Lee Lewis (Jim's personal favourite), Gene Vincent, Little Richard and, of course, Elvis Presley. I can recall us going to the local cinema in the school holidays to see *The Girl Can't Help It*, a lavish widescreen Hollywood colour movie starring Jayne Mansfield. Some cinema-goers may have been enticed along by the size of Miss Mansfield's personality, but we went several times just to catch a glimpse of artists like Eddie Cochran or Fats Domino miming to edited extracts from their recent hit recordings. We would subsequently track down all the other cheaply made black & white rock'n'roll movies of the era just to see one brief number by one of our favourites. The famous clip of Chuck Berry performing 'You Can't Catch Me' in that otherwise pretty dire Alan Freed movie *Rock, Rock, Rock* was probably one of the most thrilling and influential scenes that we ever cast eyes on. I can recall that we once hitch-hiked all the way to Bognor Regis on the South Coast simply to see the movie *Jazz On A Summer's Day*, in which Berry performed just one number.

Our investigations into obscure rock'n'roll touched on the obsessional and we soon discovered that all was not necessarily as it first seemed. Often relatively mild recordings with general teen appeal would have some meatier morsels on the 'flip'. We soon became experts at discovering the treasures that might sometimes exist on the 'B' side.

Necessity certainly does breed invention, and we needed to satisfy our insatiable curiosity with meagre resources and could not afford to squander our limited finances on mistakes. Somehow we had to find ways and means of checking out all possibilities, however unlikely or obscure. So, we consciously ingratiated ourselves with the lady who ran the record department of Rogers', the local electrical goods shop in the High Street right next to the Clock Tower. Lady? My God, she must have been all of twenty years old!

Her name was June Cutler, a slim girl with pointed features and pink highlights in her hair. Her dress code was clearly adopted from Marilyn Monroe, even though she didn't quite have the figure to match. She obviously took a shine to us and, before long, she would allow us to look through the record release sheets from the slowly increasing number of British record companies. We quickly learnt how to identify recordings with potential. For example, artists with 'teen appeal' names like Frankie Avalon and Bobby Rydell were clearly to be overlooked in favour of the likes of Screamin' Jay Hawkins or Big 'T' Tyler. Also, song titles could often be a good indication of something a little stronger. The dreaded 'A White Sport Coat (And A Pink Carnation)' was hardly going to evoke the sort of enthusiasm and anticipation we would have for titles such as 'Rumble', 'I Put A Spell On You' or 'Voodoo Voodoo', was it?

We were also suckers for any title that had Parts One and Two attached to it, for our rapidly expanding expertise led us to expect much more from such items. We soon reached the stage whereby the obliging Mrs Cutler would actually order records on our recommendation. When they arrived, she would even let us listen to them in a booth without a commitment to purchase. But occasionally we did actually deign to buy something, and this was inevitably shared around the three of us by virtue of the tape recorders.

These new and strange sounds on those American recordings were to be a big influence on Jim's musical development. It was nearly always the 'sound' that attracted him, particularly that of any unusual guitar parts. At that time, we in Britain still seemed light years behind the game with the likes of local teen heroes such as Tommy Steele who was about as threatening and dangerous as a stuffed teddy bear. How could they possibly compare with the jungle music of Bo Diddley or Little Richard?

I am afraid this is the point where my wife insists I make a confession. Being driven by the desire to hear music that was not generally broadcast on the radio, I started to find shops that sold second-hand recordings, particularly those that dealt in ex-juke box records. I found I could buy them very cheaply if I acquired a substantial batch all at once and then, with luck, we would find a few previously overlooked gems in amongst them. The problem was what to do with all the surplus duds, as most of the juke box singles were badly worn and near-white in appearance. So, I hit upon the idea of improving their immediate appearance by applying a little black shoe polish to the grooves and then washing most of it away again under the tap. On the face of it, the makeover was quite successful. So, I took to carrying a few discs around with me while walking Epsom High Street on Saturday afternoons, offering them to anyone who might care to part with a few shillings. As a consequence, it prompted one of my future wife's friends to christen me 'Sharkey', and it took me a few years to live that down. She obviously didn't appreciate polished black music or removing sticky residue from her record-player stylus.

It was around this time that Jim acquired his first electric guitar. Basically, it was a hollow-bodied acoustic model with a simple pickup, but when he attached it to a very small amplifier, it made something like the sound we all admired. I can recall that Saturday morning when I was summoned to his house to first feast eyes on it. Jim was like the cat with all the cream. Pete and I were allowed a strum, but by now we had realised that any aspirations we might have had in that direction were going to be dwarfed by Jim's talent, desire and progress. Posing in front of the wardrobe mirror with an old tennis racquet was as far as it was going to get for us two.

At this time in his life, Jim was besotted by the echo-laden sound of Scotty Moore's guitar behind Elvis Presley on those early Sun recordings. He had just about mastered most of the solos and could do a fair approximation of the two breaks in his favourite Elvis number, 'Baby Let's Play House'. Both Pete and I agreed that, to our young, enthusiastic ears, the boy sounded pretty damn good.

However attractive this initial electric model might have seemed at the time, it was only going to provide temporary satisfaction for Jim, who had by now seen photographs of exotic-shaped solid-bodied guitars with cutaway portions. It might now seem very juvenile, but all three of us collected photographs of American artists, and anyone who had an unusual-looking guitar achieved elevated status in our eyes even if, in truth, they could only manage a few chords. Incredible as it seemed to us, rock'n'roll was eventually embraced by the dear old BBC and we were even able to see the likes of Buddy Holly perform on television. When he was killed in a plane crash in 1959, I recall that Pete, Jim and I put on black ties and went to the local paper shop to buy all the newspapers that carried photos and obituaries of one of our heroes. I am sure that teenagers throughout the country felt the same sense of loss that we did.

I remember being particularly impressed when Jim manufactured an approximation of – I am reliably informed – a Fender jazz bass in his school woodwork class. He successfully copied it from a photo of the one used by Jerry Lee Lewis's bass player (apparently his father-in-law at the time) in the movie, *Disc Jockey Jamboree*. It had a particularly long neck and, while he could make the bodywork look correct, he had to compromise with the machine head and pick-up. Equipped with the right strings, though, it sounded good enough.

Apart from his brief flirtation with skiffle, Jim had not really reached the stage where he was playing with other musicians, and it was about this time that he made his first solo appearance on a children's television talent show called *All Your Own*. I reckon his mother must have been instrumental in setting it up, for she was well aware of her son's talent and gave him every encouragement. It was she who rang my father and asked if I would go with Jim to the TV studios to record the programme. The electric guitar itself was already heavy enough for him to carry, but the amplifier was like a little lead box and he clearly could not manage both. We were both skinny beanpoles in serious need of a Charles Atlas course, but I was at least a head taller than Jim and wore thick black-rimmed glasses in deference to Buddy Holly (thank God for his less-than-20/20 vision, for he gave specs some much-needed 'street cred', and none too soon as far as I was concerned). Thinking about it now, I guess I was Jim's first roadie!

We travelled by train and tube on a mid-week morning (it must have been in the school holidays) to a studio in North-West London. Jim had thoroughly rehearsed what he hoped to perform and had been trying it out on Pete and me in his front room for some weeks. Basically, he really wanted to play an instrumental, as he was never very confident about his singing. He had developed something that was roughly equivalent to the Bill Doggett r&b instrumental 'Honky Tonk' and had even given it a name. Nevertheless, he also felt that the producers would not allow him to appear without singing. He was right, of course, and in the end it proved to be a wise move that he had also rehearsed a version of 'Johnny B. Goode', which was then a fairly recent release.

When we arrived at the studios we found the place full of 'wannabes' of every shape and size. The only other musician amongst them was a child piano prodigy with blond, curly hair. This boy was probably about ten or eleven years old (at least two or three years younger than us), and therefore we pompously regarded him as just a kid. We may have thought that he resembled Shirley Temple in short trousers, but he sure could play piano. He, Jim and the others performed for a rehearsal in the morning and, as predicted, the proposed instrumental was axed.

At lunchtime, we were all invited to the canteen, but the prospect of all those precocious little stars fighting over buns and lemonade did not appeal, so we stayed behind in the studio with only the piano prodigy remaining. A little conversation took place and it transpired, much to Jim's delight, that the kid liked Jerry Lee Lewis. So, while the cats were away, the two mice had a jam. The youngster had all of Lewis's hits to date down pat! There was not too much in the way of vocals, but Jim could lay down the solos as per the records note-for-note. It may be a piece of pure fancy on my part, but I am not sure that the very talented child wasn't Roy Budd, who subsequently went on to have a successful career composing scores for films such as *Get Carter*, *Soldier Blue* and *Tomorrow Never Comes*.

When the crew returned, Jim performed 'Johnny B. Goode' in the afternoon and was briefly interviewed by the programme presenter, Huw Weldon, who subsequently went on to become the head of the British Broadcasting Corporation. (To progress from being a children's television presenter to head of one of the most powerful and influential broadcasting organisations in the world might have seemed a bit far-fetched at the time, but I guess Ronald Reagan was still riding his horse in cowboy movies in those days.)

We enjoyed our day out in the big time and eventually viewed the results in small screen black & white one Sunday evening some weeks later. Jim's mum seemed suitably pleased.

To say Jim was dedicated would be an understatement. I hardly ever saw him when he wasn't strapped to his guitar trying to figure out some new licks. Strange as it may seem, his main source of inspiration at the time came via a clean-cut pop idol. Ricky Nelson was the product of a famous US television family and, despite his pointed nose (he never seemed to be photographed side on), he looked every inch the polite young man. However, young Mr Nelson clearly had a love of rockabilly and it was later revealed that his own personal favourite was Carl Perkins, who was certainly far more rough and tough by comparison. Ricky's teen ballads sold well enough in Britain, but it was the rocking 'B' sides featuring guitarist James Burton that really appealed to Jim. Those old Nelson records might seem pretty tame now, but back then the guitar solos (including the ones played by Joe Maphis) were cutting-edge stuff and greatly impressed my pal. I remember that he struggled for a long time with the instrumental break of 'It's Late', but eventually someone showed him the fingerings he was after and he happily moved on.

* * *

III

As my father probably needed a break from the incessant noise coming from my record player, he would occasionally farm me out to his sisters who lived in Bayswater in West London. There, I learnt a little more about life as I ogled the young maids who worked in my aunts' nursing home and began to understand why those fancy-smelling women would constantly walk their poodles up and down the paths in nearby Hyde Park. In the big city, I could explore even more second-hand shops and, on Jim's behalf, duly found loads of cheap and fairly nasty Ricky Nelson albums that had a few tracks with a good solo here and there. Jim would lap these up, and you could tell where the good parts were by just looking at the disc, for they were the portions being worn white.

The next step on our learning ladder came with the opening of a rock'n'roll club in Epsom. Actually, it was just a regular dance that took place on Friday evenings at the Ebisham Hall in the centre of town. Nevertheless, it gloried in the grand title of the 'Contemporary Club', which now seems laughable. At this stage, we were still too young to attend (and didn't have enough money to get in anyway), but we would hang around the rear fire exit doors next to the stage to hear the bands, most of which were pretty routine except for Chris Farlowe & The Thunderbirds. This group seriously impressed us, and eventually Jim would strike up a long and lasting friendship with the leader, whose real name was John Deighton (or 'Tubby' as he was affectionately known in those days).

Jim longed for a band to play with, so he set about organising his own. He found a guy from nearby Banstead who could sing and play rhythm guitar, but unfortunately he didn't really have very much feel for pulsating rock'n'roll. Jim also recruited a spotty-faced lad who could play piano, and eventually preparations were made for their first ever professional gig.

By this time I guess I was approaching sixteen and girls had definitely come into the frame. On Saturday afternoons the town's youth had taken to congregating at the Clock Tower in the centre of town. Here, greasy Norman Evans would incessantly run a comb through his locks, the Jelly sisters would increase male pulse rates, and 'Terry the Diesel' would make fictitious adjustments to his BSA motorbike.

It so happened that on one weekend my father was away visiting his sisters. In a fit of euphoria, I spread the news that there would be a party at my house that evening. It wasn't until later in the day that I remembered that it was also the night of Jim's gig. I instantly abandoned plans for the proposed party and went around to Jim's house to be a roadie without wheels again.

We gathered in his front room as usual and were just about to leave when there was a knock at the door. Jim opened up and found two girls on the doorstep who insisted they had been invited to a party at my house. They had found my place in darkness, but, as they walked back to the main road along the crescent, they spied us in Jim's front room. It may have been embarrassing, but it was a fair cop, so we invited them to come along with us to Jim's first ever paid gig at the Comrades' Club.

The venue was a small war veterans' drinking club near the centre of the town, and even though we were all under-age, we managed to get in as part of the band. There is no way to describe this event in a flattering light, for the gig was a complete shambles. The elderly Comrades would clearly have preferred a traditional dance band to perform well-known numbers that they could dance to if they so chose. As it was, Jim and his two buddies had no name for the band, no drummer and really only played rock'n'roll. Somehow, we managed to buy drinks and started to try out our best chat-up lines on the girls. To their credit, the three debutant musicians tried their best to keep the small crowd happy. After a very short first set there was a break in which the young pianist started to play solo a few of the old favourites that the Comrades might appreciate on the upright piano. This was potentially a smart move, but it soon became obvious that he was being bought drinks by the patrons and was getting very drunk, very quickly.

The two girls tried to appear nonchalant about the whole affair, but the outcome soon seemed inevitable. The dark haired one, Anna, was very tasty and both Jim and I fancied her. But meanwhile our piano man had got very agitated and we could see that trouble was on its way. Jim and I either drew straws or made a pact, but one way or the other it ended up with him bundling his gear and the drunk into a taxi and me taking Anna home. I guess that evening shaped the rest of my life, although that's another story – but thanks, Jim, just the same!

* * *

IV

Jim and I continued to frequent the record shop in town. One afternoon, June Cutler introduced us to her husband, who was, shall we say, *unusual*. He seemed to us to be quite a bit older than her and had obviously had an accident somewhere down the line, for he had an artificial hand. His wife's profession and the emergence of rock'n'roll might have brought out his entrepreneurial instincts, for he decided to have a go at being a music promoter. He found a willing participant and tried to manufacture his own rock'n'roll prodigy, whom he named Billy Scarlet. June insisted we go and see the wonder boy perform one night in the nearby village of Ashtead. How could we refuse? She was the hand that fed us the music we craved…so we dutifully attended. Unfortunately, the bespectacled young aspirant turned out to be a Cliff Richard clone with an inept band. Although we all thought that he wasn't much of a singer, we had to agree that his blood-red jacket did look damn impressive. I think that may have been Mr Cutler's first and last attempt at becoming an rock'n'roll impresario.

It is safe to say that what Jim really yearned for most at this time in his life was a solid-body Fender guitar like the ones we had seen in the photos of our American heroes. As chance would have it, his dream was almost in reach. In those far-off days there used to be an annual exhibition at Olympia in Earls Court in West London called *The Radio Show*, or something similarly quaint. Pete Neal decided that the three of us should go, if for no other reason that it was away from Epsom and we could at least practise our attempts at picking up girls. We went on the train and spent the day browsing around dozens of boring exhibits that mainly catered for adults with disposable incomes way beyond ours.

However, there was one stand where live music was performed. People from the audience were invited to get up and sing, and I think I can best describe the accompanying musicians as a nightclub trio. It attracted a reasonable crowd and we watched while a then-unknown schoolboy called Laurie London got up to sing a number. He would very soon record a catchy religious song called 'He's Got The Whole World In His Hands' and briefly become a household name on the back of it.

Jim watched along with us, but he was transfixed by something other than the vocalists, for the journeyman singer/guitarist in the backing trio was playing a Fender Telecaster. It was the first time we had ever laid eyes on one in the flesh, as it were. That was it as far as Jim was concerned, for he was now determined to actually touch the object of his desire.

He made us hang around for what seemed like hours while he patiently waited in line to get up on the stage and perform a number. Eventually his turn came and the reluctant musician allowed him to briefly borrow the Telecaster and render a rock'n'roll number – 'Down The Line', if I recall correctly. There was only polite applause, but Jim didn't care, for he had actually laid his hands on a Fender for the first time! On the way home on the train, he was like a dog with two tails.

Although the day when Jim would actually own his Fender was still a little way off, it was not long before he managed to acquire a Grazziola (it sounds like something off a pizza menu!) copycat Fender-style guitar complete with a tremolo arm, or what would later become known as a 'whammy bar'. The music shops in London's Charing Cross Road were at last beginning to wake up to what the new generation wanted.

Now Jim at least looked the part, and he started to develop his rocker dress sense. Pegged black trousers, winklepicker shoes and a vertical striped jacket were generally the order of the day. The three of us must have spent hours in front of the mirror combing our hair into extravagant elephant trunks. Clearly, I must have been too diligent, for, less than ten years later, there wasn't a single strand left on my forehead.

To his credit, Jim was undaunted by the catastrophe at the Comrades' Club, and the next step had to be an appearance at the aforementioned Contemporary Club. By now we had managed to gain entry, and were at least known to the guy who ran the place and his fierce-looking Alsatian dog. The venue may have had a pretentious name, but it was nothing more than a large meeting hall with a wooden-boarded floor. It wasn't licensed, so there was no bar, but on Friday nights the stable lads from the nearby Downs would come into town and get drunk in the pub next door. By closing time, the bouncers were almost always called into action to break up the fights with the local boys. We three came for the music and the girls and skilfully managed to avoid the mayhem. Anna and her friends attended regularly, so we were never short of dance partners. Apart from the revered Chris Farlowe, one of the other bands to regularly appear was an early version of the Dave Clark Five, though this was well before their rise to international fame. We enjoyed them, but they were not really down

Red. E. Lewis & The Redcaps in action.
Left to right: Jumbo, Red and Jim.

and dirty enough for our tastes.

Somehow, Jim convinced the boss man to give him and his group a chance to open for one of the featured bands. It was a much-anticipated event for us and, of course, we turned up to provide some support. Jim had found a halfway decent drummer and, although he persevered with the singer, I remember it as a primarily instrumental set. If I also remember correctly, Jim's mother and father were ushered into the back of the hall and discretely witnessed their son's initial efforts from wooden chairs at the rear. The place was by no means full as the young band took the stage early in the evening, but, given the circumstances, they did just fine and were well received.

Jim's playing dominated proceedings of course, and his version of 'Red River Rock' impressed everyone including the singer with the featured band, who was standing next to me near the front of the stage. This gentleman's stage name was Red E. Lewis and his band were called the Redcaps. He was the archetypal rocker of the period, who did indeed have red hair that was extravagantly swept back into a D.A. (that's 'duck's arse', for those of you too young to remember). The guy seemed to have a complete Gene Vincent fixation, but it must be said that, despite their name, his band was not quite up to the job. That situation was about to change for, although he may have looked a trifle Neanderthal, he was certainly no fool and he recognised Jim's talent immediately. The band's manager was informed and it was only a matter of weeks before Jim was the new lead guitarist with the Redcaps. I doubt if he was much more than sixteen years old, but he was now on his way.

The band was managed by a young Londoner named Chris Tidmarsh, who was very mature for his years. We were all pretty impressed by him, not just because he seemed older, but we could see that he was a handsome, well-dressed guy and a very smooth operator.

The guys in the group were easy to get on with, particularly Jumbo, the new bass player, whose real name was John Spicer. Not that he actually played bass at the time – he just filled in the rhythm pattern on second guitar. He was a bit weighty, hence the nickname, and had a mop of curly ginger hair. Jumbo also had a great natural sense of humour that was a much-needed asset, as Red was rather one-dimensional. I think it's fair to say that Jim very soon became the musical arranger for the band. That does sound rather grand, for, at that point, his contribution was probably to ensure that they all stopped playing at roughly the same time.

V

Time moved on and I left school at the age of sixteen. I was hardly an outstanding student, and coming from a relatively poor household, my father reckoned I needed a career-type job that would enable me to earn a reasonable income in future years. I was pretty good at mathematics and, for some reason, he decided I should be a surveyor. Well, it sounded posh, didn't it, but I was only really interested in parties and music, and if getting a job didn't get in the way of those pursuits, then so be it.

It must have been my dad's efforts that got me my first job with a building contactor based in Putney, in South London. I turned up the first day in a shirt, tie and dogtooth check jacket feeling quite the young businessman. I spent the first few weeks filing drawings and checking someone's calculations (electronic calculators had yet to come on the market) while trying to chat up the girls in the typing pool. It all seemed a doddle until they sent me off to be based on a housing development site near Bromley in Kent and the real world came down on me like a proverbial ton of bricks. This is where my education in 'life' really began.

I may have had the fancy title of Junior Assistant Surveyor, but I was in fact just the 'gofer' for the site manager. He was man named White, an ex-sergeant major with dreadful halitosis who ran the place like the war was still taking place. Everyone called him Whitey, but only behind his back. He was a failed military dictator with absolutely no sense of humour, and I had to learn fast how to just exist in his presence.

The one thing that changed radically in those first few months was my behaviour and language. Up until then I guess I was a relatively polite young man, but that was to be short lived. The phone would ring in the site office and Whitey would tell me to go over to block three and tell Mr Smith, the subcontractor bricklayer boss, he was wanted on the phone. I would see him a few floors up on the scaffold and politely call out, 'Excuse me, Mr Smith, there is a phone call for you!' But there would be no response. After about five minutes of repeated attempts to gain his attention, I heard Whitey's foot steps behind me. 'Oi, fuckin' Smiffy,' he bellowed, 'You're wanted on the fuckin' blower!' And, wondrously, Mr Smith's response was immediate.

I soon learnt that, in order to communicate on site, you had to use a special kind of punctuation. Instead of full stops and commas, you had to use the magic all-purpose word 'fucking' – without the 'g', preferably – as loud as you could manage, and as often as possible. A ratio of about one word in every three was about right. The full awareness of this new form of communication fully dawned on me a few weeks later.

One afternoon, Whitey had gone off site and left me to mind the office. I gazed out the window and daydreamed about those women walking their poodles in the park until I noticed that the company plant manager had arrived on site. He was a great fat balloon of a man and he was making his way towards the central concrete mixer. I could see that he was gesticulating at the operator and his body language was not that of a happy bunny. He turned in my direction and his face was bright red as he made his way towards the office steps. Even an inexperienced youth such as I knew it was time to get my head down into some papers and look busy. The door burst open. He thundered into the office, slumped into a chair and uttered the following immortal sentence: 'Fuck the fuckin' fucker, he's fucked the fuckin' thing again!'

For a moment the world stood still while I took in the full significance of this highly original piece of prose. Yes, it did make some sense, and I guessed that the concrete mixer driver was not going to be in our employment, or perhaps even this world, for much longer.

As it happened, the poor man did keep his job. The dozy sod had let the concrete set inside the mixer drum. His job-saving task was to sit inside the huge metal canister and break out the now-hard concrete with a mechanical hammer and without the aid of ear mufflers. If he did have just a few healthy brain cells before he started, he certainly had them well scrambled by the time he had finished.

On another enlightening occasion, I discovered that a single, well-chosen noun could mean more than one might first assume. There was a site meeting taking place in the office, when there was a loud knock on the door. Whitey gestured for me to go and deal with the matter. I opened the door, and there in front of me was the most gigantic black man. He was so large he almost blocked out all the daylight. He looked at me from beneath a huge hat and uttered just one word: 'Shit.'

I was dumbstruck. He looked at me as if I was in a trance and repeated the word even louder. I stood there frozen until I felt Whitey's hand on my shoulder. He pulled me to one side, and pointed to the mess room and told the giant that it was the second door on the right. Enlightenment dawned about the same time as the red blood reached the surface of the skin on my cheeks and I learnt another lesson in brief phraseology.

All this was the beginning of the end of any semblance of decorum in my life. I found that the 'word' crept into my conversation almost all the time – and not only when I was on site. On one memorable occasion, my father and I went to tea at my Aunt Maud's and when asked if I liked the cake, I replied that I thought it was 'fuckin' wonderful'. My father was not amused.

But I digress. Let us get back to discovering music.

VI

I was seeing Anna on a regular basis now, and we would go to the band's gigs and just generally hang out with them. The group had bookings all around London and the Southern Counties, and we would sometimes tag along in the van. Jumbo was not a particularly gifted musician, but he was a very friendly guy and he and Jim got on exceptionally well. He was certainly not resentful when Jim became the natural driving force behind the band's primitive but developing musical arrangements.

Me and Jumbo on the beach at Climping.

I well remember when they went on holiday together to Littlehampton on the South Coast. I think they had a chalet next to Jumbo's parents at some small holiday camp. They took their new suits and winklepicker shoes with them and certainly spent more time in the town's tiny Top Hat nightclub trying to impress the local girls than sunning themselves on the beach. However, we did go down to visit them for the day, and stuck in an old photo album I still have some tiny black & white photos of us lounging around in the sand dunes at Climping. Back in those days, it was an attractive spot on the South Coast, but I could not really recommend it to you now. Anna recently went there for a walk with a girlfriend and was saddened to discover that it is now a rampant gay pick-up area.

Despite all my musical involvement with Jim, it is Anna who can claim to have arguably played the most critical part in his life and this is her favourite after- dinner story concerning him.

Although Jim was regularly playing with the group, we continued to jointly pursue our obsession with 'our' music. Through the grapevine we learned of a forthcoming Jerry Lee Lewis gig at a venue in nearby Croydon. At that time, 'The Killer' could do no wrong as far as Jim was concerned, and I got us a couple of tickets well in advance. Unfortunately, when the gig finally came around, I was laid up in bed with a nasty dose of glandular fever and only felt like dying. It was agreed that Anna would go along with Jim, rather than waste the spare ticket. I have heard the story many times, and the way Anna tells it, her prompt actions safely ensured the birth of heavy metal.

Apparently, the concert was at a regular theatre and their seats were in the front row of the upstairs balcony. Jerry Lee eventfully came on and really got into his usual barnstorming act. According to Anna, Jim was rather enthusiastic and spent most of the set standing on his seat. It was when Jerry approached the crescendo of his performance and climbed upon the piano that Anna started to become concerned. It seems that Jim was similarly inspired and was now precariously perched with his feet on the top of the balcony barrier. Anna was sure he, delirious with joy, was about to topple into the stalls below. Thankfully for all those later-to-be metal maniacs, Jim was wearing a belted jacket. And so, with his wellbeing in mind, she clung on to it desperately until Jerry Lee finally left the stage. Jim would have been on his own 'stairway to heaven' there and then if hadn't been for my dear wife, and I am sure that the future sales of the Gibson Les Paul would have been paltry by comparison. There are, of course, some who might say that she has quite a lot to answer for...

Performing with the Redcaps meant that Jim would get to know the bands that played at the Contemporary and other venues in the London area. Thus, he was soon able to meet Chris Farlowe and his band, the Thunderbirds, whom we admired so much. I even remember us all travelling in the van on a night off to see them play at some far-off gig in Essex.

Jim really enjoyed watching lead guitarist Bobby Taylor, who had a unique style of playing. Jimmy's admiration was such that I am almost sure that he and another friend from nearby Stoneleigh put up some of there own money, so that Tubby and the band could record an album in a local studio. I remember that there were only a few copies pressed and we would listen to it intently in Jim's front room.

I think that there were ten tracks and two of them were instrumentals featuring Bobby Taylor. One of these was a version of a Les McCann early jazz-funk style number called 'Fish This Week', or something like that. Jim was mightily impressed, and played it over and over again. I have to say that, from my point of view, I was much more impressed with Tubby's vocals, for he had a real feel for the music. I particularly enjoyed his treatment of the Carl Perkins version of 'Matchbox', where he would scat-sing along with Bobby's solo. Yes, they were a groundbreaking band who were really ahead of their time, and sadly they didn't receive the recognition they deserved when the blues explosion eventually hit Britain a few years later.

Even at this early stage, Jim was getting into the idea of improving the impact of his playing by recording and amplification techniques. I remember during our constant exploration we found a record which included a distinctly fuzzy guitar tone and were blissfully unaware that this was caused by a simple piece of amplification kit that you just could not yet buy in Britain. Incredible as it may seem, Jim even experimented with an elastic band around the fret board like a capo to see if he could reproduce that sound. Needless to say he was unsuccessful and couldn't keep the guitar in tune. For Jim, it was all about new sounds, and when he discovered the work of Chet Atkins he immediately wanted to acquire a foot pedal. I also remember how taken he was with Link Wray's 'Rumble', though the idea of puncturing the amp speaker with pinholes passed him by.

In order to try out all these techniques and get some idea of how they sounded, he convinced his parents to buy him an expensive multi- (well, maybe four-) track tape recorder. With this new tool, he could undertake some crude recording and overdubbing in that tiny front room. He could readily lay down the guitar parts but, having no drum kit, the rhythm was added by him slapping his knees or playing with drumsticks on a cardboard box. It was usually all just recorded directly through the tape machine microphone.

One day, in an uncharacteristic fit of artistic endeavour, I wrote a simple song and called it 'I'm Slipping Into Your Heart', and nervously sang it to Jim. I am sure it was almost completely devoid of any tune. To my amazement and pleasure Jim agreed to toy with it. So, I wrote down the lyrics, and a few weeks later he presented me with a small reel of tape with him performing the number with a suitable and very typically distorted guitar solo. If only I had safely stored that little tape, its auction on eBay might have proved interesting! In reality, I suspect it somehow got lost when I stored my few possessions before I left to travel overseas. In my dreams I might have aspired to being Leiber or Stoller, but it was never to be. Many years later I gave it a try just once more, and the New York singer/guitarist Larry Dale did record a blues 'wot I done wrote', but to this date it has remained in the can – which is probably the best place for it.

It would be a gross understatement to say that the performances of Red E. Lewis & The Redcaps were enhanced by Jim's presence, but it was clear that this band had limited horizons with the incumbent singer. The manager, Chris Tidmarsh, was nothing if not ambitious and I'm sure it was not many months before Big Red was given the equally large elbow. Again, I am not exactly sure of the timing of these events, but I guess it was in late '61 or early '62. I don't know how Chris met the replacement singer, but I believe he found him while visiting the 2I's coffee bar in Soho. Anyway, he was introduced to me as Smokey Dean, and the band adopted a new name: the Dean Aces.

VII

Smokey was an interesting character to say the least. He spoke with an American accent, which we all thought was phoney, but it eventually transpired that he may indeed have come from the good old USA. On the face of it, I guess he was much better looking than ol' Red and therefore more marketable, but that wasn't saying much. Anna was convinced his slicked-back blond hair was dyed and wasn't sure about him. One night when he borrowed my jacket to wear on stage I began to get a bit wary myself. During the break, Jim took me aside and urged me to ensure that I got it back after the show.

The band's rock'n'roll repertoire hardly changed, but at least they had a slightly more presentable singer out front. Jim would tell me amusing stories about Smokey. Most people who knew him thought him to be a pathological liar because he always had some far-fetched tale to tell. However, Jim was never entirely certain how to judge his tall stories because there was always a grain of truth that put doubt in the mind.

Our view of him is summed up by one particular occasion when he returned from a trip to America. Being aware of Jim's fascination with the James Burton solos on those early Ricky Nelson singles, he informed us that he had heard a new recording of Nelson performing 'Milk Cow Blues' while in the States. We dismissed this as typical Smokey bullshit, for by now Ricky had changed record companies, his name had become plain and simple 'Rick', and he was recording a succession of boring ballads for the increasingly conservative US market. However, a month or so later, the song was actually issued in Britain on a Decca subsidiary as the 'B' side of 'Fools Rush In'. I am not sure if we were more surprised that Nelson was still continuing to record such material, or to discover that Smokey was actually telling the truth. Either way, Jim was well pleased with the record, for it did indeed have the typical Burton trademark guitar-work.

I have to confess that I am not sure of all the details to do with the following, but the timescale appears to fit. As Smokey had a reputation for telling woppers, it's not surprising that we didn't believe him when he told us that he had previously had a record released in Britain. Here he was, gigging in small-time local dancehalls where nobody on this circuit had got a record out, not even Chris Farlowe. The general feeling was just to ignore his claims. However, either he or Chris

Tidmarsh must have had some good connections, for it wasn't long before the prospect of recording became a real possibility. The home market for local, rather than imported American talent was beginning to blossom. I recall being quite impressed when Jim told me that they were rehearsing and that Smokey was going to cut a record. Although it did take place, the record didn't get released under the name Smokey Dean, with or without the Dean Aces.

The songs that Smokey was due to record were 'Blowing Wild', plus a version of 'Ubangi Stomp', an old Jerry Lee Lewis number that the band had recently adopted. I think the then-prolific Joe Meek may have been the engineer involved, but I am less sure if Jim actually played on the studio session. He would have been perfect for the occasion, of course, but this may have been his first experience of the closed-shop sessionman mafia that prevailed at the time. Many working bands had been subjected to the old boys' act when their time came to record, and the regular band members were excluded from the vocalist's recordings in a none-too-subtle manner. The impending popularity of groups like the Beatles and the Stones would soon make this practice obsolete, but, if Jim did indeed play on 'Ubangi Stomp', it would have been his first-ever studio session.

It wasn't long before the record was issued on the HMV label – under the name 'Dean Shannon'. I didn't realise it at the time, but the reason for this apparent name change was that the enigmatic Smokey had indeed recorded a single ('Blinded With Love' *b/w* a rocked-up version of 'Jezebel') for the same label a couple of years earlier. He was probably still under contract to the company as 'Dean Shannon'. Yet again, his tall tales appeared to have some real fabric.

Chris Tidmarsh was never slow to see some advantage, so now his act was promoted as 'HMV recording star, Dean Shannon', but I don't think the band knew how to play the awful 'Blowing Wild', and I am sure I never heard them perform it. In any case, the association with Mr Shannon didn't last very much longer. I can only apply conjecture, but I am sure the shrewd young Mr Tidmarsh must have thought that 'anything he can do, I can do just as well'. That would not have been far from the truth, for Smokey wasn't exactly a great singer. A swift transition took place, with a new bid for stardom. Chris may not have had much of a voice, but he must have had a burning ambition, for he literally pushed himself to the fore to become the new vocalist and leader of the group.

I was present at his debut, and his extreme nervousness lingers in

Neil Christian & The Crusaders backstage at the Edmonton Regal, 1960.
Left to right: Jim, drummer Jimmy Evans, Neil Christian and Jumbo.

the mind. As I have said before, he was a good-looking guy, and he certainly knew how to present himself in a manner that would be attractive to the girls. Much care was taken in the choice of the clothes that he wore on stage, and by this time he had the luxury of a cracking red-hot rock'n'roll band to back him up and paper over any cracks. Accordingly, Neil Christian & The Crusaders were born.

It is remiss of me that I have neglected to mention one very significant event for Jim during this period. He at last managed to achieve one of his early goals and become the proud owner of a Fender Stratocaster. It was not a garish colour, but the standard sunburst model we had so long admired in the photographs of American artists. I can clearly remember the first time that I saw him use it for a gig. Perhaps it was because he knew that Pete and I were watching, but he was like a kid at Christmas with the best present possible. His excessive use of the tremolo arm that night was entirely understandable and we shared in his obvious pleasure.

Strange as it might seem, however, he didn't really use the Fender for that long with the Crusaders. When Chris took over vocal duties, the band soon got more frequent (and presumably lucrative) gigs. Jim was probably making a healthy income for a young man still living at his parents' house, so it was not long before he graduated to a Gretsch guitar. The instrument had become suddenly fashionable here with Eddie Cochran's visit to Britain. Jim admired Cochran greatly, and many of his numbers were used in Neil Christian's act. He liked both the sound and appearance of the instrument that had also been made popular by Chet Atkins. My expertise in such things is minimal, but I think this particular model was called a 'Country Gentleman'. If my memory is correct, the colour of Jim's chosen instrument was exactly the same as the warm orange-tinted one that appeared on the cover of the Atkins album that Jim owned. He certainly admired the Atkins style of country picking and his 'Trambone' was a regular practice-piece for Jim at home. There is absolutely no doubt that the rockabilly style of playing was Jim's first love in those years.

I don't think that anyone was under the illusion that Neil Christian (as I shall refer to him from now on) was a gifted singer, least of all himself. The sort of music the band were performing required style and excitement, for, in most cases, the audiences were dancers who demanded familiar songs. Nevertheless, the guys took nothing for granted, and I think a conscious effort was made to develop a dynamic act that covered up some of their singer's shortcomings. They presented themselves in a professional, businesslike manner, but were not too proud to copy other bands such as Johnny Kidd & The Pirates. His 'Shakin' All Over' was a very popular number which the guys had down verbatim and embellished their performance with high leg-kicks to match the stop time tempo breaks.

The band had always worn uniforms, but now everyone took more care. Neil was very fastidious about his appearance and I can remember him being particularly proud of being featured in a rag trade magazine, *Tailor & Cutter*. He was shown wearing a classic city gent's business suit and was described as a particularly well dressed up-and-coming pop star.

Even back in the days of Red E. Lewis, the slow, bluesy Gene Vincent number 'Baby Blue' had been the highlight of the group's performance. With Jim at the helm, the band developed the tune into Neil Christian's trademark number. The song had natural tension anyway, but the guys would do everything possible to accentuate the impact. All members, apart from the drummer, would lie down on the floor during Jim's emotional and protracted guitar solo, and every drop of drama was regularly milked.

Unfortunately, the song was becoming so popular that several other bands were using it as well. So, in a typically shrewd move (pre-dating any similar Zeppelin activities by several years), they decided to dump the song in favour of an old New Orleans rhythm & blues hit called

'One Night'. The song was originally recorded by Smiley Lewis, but had been more recently modified into a more universally acceptable vehicle for Elvis Presley. Adult lines such as *'One night of sin is what I'm now paying for'* were replaced with *'One night with you is what I'm now praying for'*, in typical Hollywood fashion, for teen audience consumption. The guys kept the 'Baby Blue'-style arrangement and gave the number exactly the same all-fall-down treatment. With its more appealing lyric and Neil's good looks, the song did have a pretty mesmerising effect on the girls who were now beginning to gather regularly at the front of the stage.

Now, I have to tell you that the gathering of these girls was not exactly a spontaneous event. I would not like to swear who organised it, but some enthusiastic young ladies were brought along to a few gigs on the understanding that they must have a good scream in front of the stage at the height of Chris's act. Such staged histrionics, however phoney, did nothing to diminish Mr Christian's reputation.

I think the change from 'Baby Blue' to 'One Night' was the dawning of the need to perform numbers that were different from the well-known hits that were trotted out mechanically by the other bands on the circuit. Prompted by this requirement, Jim would studiously search our record collections for obscure numbers that he thought Neil might be able to handle. The most memorable of these was 'Watch Your Step'.

Jim and I were still going into the record shop in the town, taking advantage of June Cutler's good nature, and when we found the Bobby Parker song listed, it did sound like a good title. The record was duly ordered, and when it arrived we played it in the shop. We didn't get thirty seconds into it before we were blown away. This was *exactly* the sort of record that we had been searching for! That stunning guitar intro, based on Ray Charles's 'What'd I Say', was so exciting, and the gospel-styled vocal and incoherent lyrics matched the mood perfectly. We regarded this as a treasured find and played it to death, including the equally strong blues on the flip side, 'Steal Your Heart Away', which was also based on a Charles song, 'I Believe To My Soul'. It proved a perfect vehicle for Neil Christian, for, although his vocal abilities were tame by comparison to Parker, the excitement that the number carried with it was all that was needed to make it a dancehall favourite. Zeppelin fans might be interested in another reincarnation of 'Watch Your Step', but more of that later.

VIII

Meanwhile, at the sharp end of things, my building site experiences were quickly giving me a crash course in a side of life I could never have imagined a few months earlier. The job I was working on was a fairly substantial housing project with a large labour force where personnel of all kinds seem to come and go on a regular basis. In those days there was little in the way of sophisticated machinery and the strip foundations for the residential blocks were dug out by hand. Often, a piece work gang of Irish labourers would be involved and invariably they would work hard all week and then go to the pub at midday on Friday. As a result mayhem would often occur during the subsequent afternoon. Whitey would fire individuals on a regular basis and they would have to come back the next site payday, a Thursday, and collect the cash owing to them. Many a fierce argument would take place on those Thursday afternoons.

On one occasion, an Irish labourer had a falling-out with his colleagues and became so incensed that he went in a fit of anger into the adjacent nearby building shell, climbed to the second floor and started throwing breeze blocks out of the window onto his workmates. Sgt White was informed, and after a none-too-friendly altercation, the labourer was sacked on the spot. On the following Thursday, Whitey was conspicuously absent for most of the day and I was left alone in the office to deal with whatever crisis might occur… Which, it transpired, was the sacked Irishman, who staggered up the steps at two o'clock in search of his wages.

I answered a knock on the office door and there was the labourer swaying in front of me. In popular modern day parlance, he was pissed out of his brain. His bloodshot eyes met mine and he said, 'I've come for me money.'

'I'm sorry,' I stammered, 'but the money is not due here until three o'clock.'

'I want my money,' was his angry reply.

'Well, if you come back at three o'clock, sir, I am sure the money will be here.'

Then he uttered a few words that I shall remember until my dying day: 'What time at tree o'clock shall I come for me money?'

It was then that my eyes settled on a milk bottle protruding from the man's torn jacket pocket, and I believe that the passage of time then became suspended in that part of South-East London. Thankfully, my mind eventually engaged and I shrewdly reasoned that the milk bottle was not there to provide him with calcium sustenance. *Choose your next words carefully*, I thought, for I felt that the merest twitch at the corner of my lips, let alone a smile or a laugh, would result – if I survived – in a visit to the hospital to have glass extracted from my skull. I have no recollection of how I replied, but whatever it was it did the job, for he turned around and staggered off.

These were probably my earliest attempts at diplomacy.

Indeed, there was a lot I needed to learn, for I was incredibly naïve. One day, I was chatting to the woman who ran the site canteen and remarked that I was surprised to see that one of the guys digging in the foundations had dirty jeans and boots on, but was wearing a smart three button jacket with a folded handkerchief and what looked like a polished envelope opener in his top pocket.

'Oh, that's Mickey,' she replied.

'Oh, yes?' was my quizzical response.

She then told me that this smart gentleman was in fact 'Mickey the Dagger' and that the ornament in his pocket was indeed a paper knife with both edges sharpened like a razor. Apparently, he had a reputation for using it throughout the neighbourhood – and not for opening letters with. I took in a deep breath and decided to give Mr Mickey a wide berth.

About two weeks later, three police cars came screeching into the site entrance interrupting a boring afternoon. Out poured a pile of coppers who ran towards the new foundations. I looked out the side window and there was Mickey in his posh jacket making a dash for the opposite site boundary fence. Thankfully, he did not come back on the following Thursday for his money.

The police were fairly regular visitors to the site once the buildings started to contain elements that were worth stealing. I remember Whitey complaining that we were missing quite a lot of sanitary fittings and he could not find out how they were being taken. He would instruct me to go to the top of the tallest block at the end of each day and watch the workmen leave the site to see if I could spot anything suspicious. At knocking off time, they all poured out of the site and I saw nothing unusual until I got bored and started to look at the vista around me. Suddenly, I saw something very strange in the fields behind the site. There seemed to be two huge tortoises lumbering across the fields towards a copse of bushes. *Wait a minute*, I reasoned, *these aren't reptiles; they are upturned baths with human arms and legs!* I reported my find to Whitey and he went over to the copse, via a hole that had been cut in the site boundary fence. There he discovered a hidden stash of his missing sanitary fittings waiting to be taken away at some later date. Whitey made another of his calls to the cops and a few days later, the human tortoises were caught red-handed.

It was virtually impossible to stop petty pilfering of small items that could be carried away in a toolbag. I had a similar holdall in which I carried books to study on the long boring train journey to and from my place of work. One evening, I rushed from the site to catch my train and as I ran up the street my bag seemed to weigh a ton. When I reached the train, I was exhausted. I sat down and opened the bag to find that some wag had put a couple of bricks in there with my books. I left them under the seat for the cleaner to take home.

IX

One day, Jim, who was getting to know more and more musicians on the circuit, invited me to go with him to meet another equally young guitarist named Mick Green who was just starting out on his career with Johnny Kidd & The Pirates. Jim clearly felt a musical affinity with Mick and was very impressed with his very personal style of playing. So, on a mid-week evening, we travelled by train and tube to Southfields, near Wimbledon in South London, where Mick lived with his parents. Their home was in a large block of flats and, although the two guitarists' jamming was very low key, I couldn't help but hope that the neighbours appreciated their endeavours.

Although their playing together was enjoyable – for Mick had a quite unusual rhythmic approach to solos – it was something unexpected that remains in my memory of the evening. Mick eventually got round to telling us about his initial motivation to play guitar. He told us that his father had taught him the basics from an early age and that his dad had played in the Post Office Banjo Band. What, a banjo band? This really intrigued me, and I was seriously impressed when Mick produced a photograph of the ensemble. There seemed to be twenty or more guys posed in rows like a football team, all with banjos of different sizes. My God, they must have made a din, for the banjo is one loud instrument and there were some very large ones on display! I guess our four-piece rock'n'roll groups were really just the equivalent of our parents' massed banjo bands. I still chuckle when I think about it.

It seemed inevitable that it would happen, and sometime in 1962 Neil Christian cut his first record for Columbia: 'The Road To Love' *b/w* 'The Big Beat Drum'. Again, I'm sure that it was sessionmen rather than the regular band on those studio recordings, but that notwithstanding, the group had a strong bond with a well worked-out act, and by now were getting some pretty good gigs. Occasionally these were in bizarre locations, and I was surprised when Anna informed me that the boys were playing at the Harrodian Club.

At that time, Anna was working for the internationally-known Harrods Group, but the club was not at their famous Knightsbridge store. The company had a warehouse at Barnes in West London, overlooking the River Thames. We turned up at this large, faded but 'rather grand looking' two-storey building and eventually found that the gig was in the basement. Apparently, the event was intended as some kind of staff jolly, but it was not very well attended. However, this social club must have been well funded, even in the years before Mr Al Fayed. There were two featured bands and, while the opening act were thrashing away, we went backstage to see the guys and admire Jumbo's new cherry-red Burns guitar that he had just acquired.

While we were chatting, Jim introduced us to a guy who was going to perform a couple of numbers with the group. It initially seemed strange that Neil would allow anyone else to appear with his group, but he was a sharp guy and surely wasn't going to let anyone steal his spotlight. Any doubts on my part were dispelled when it was revealed that this guy was a contemporary poet who intended to get up and spout verse while Jim and the boys provided some instrumental accompaniment. Eventually, the band took the stage and after a few warm-up numbers the bearded poet was introduced (facial hair was regarded as somewhat abnormal in those days). He rendered some vaguely provocative verses about nipples, thighs and pubic hair while the group played Shadows-style instrumentals. It was hardly a roaring success, but the poet didn't seem to mind. He was possibly a few years too premature, for he would have probably gone down a bundle at the Isle of Wight or Woodstock a few years later.

We retreated backstage again at the conclusion of the set and the poet introduced himself as Royston Ellis, and explained that he was touring the country trying his luck with all sorts of groups. He told us that he was going north to Liverpool next and was going to perform

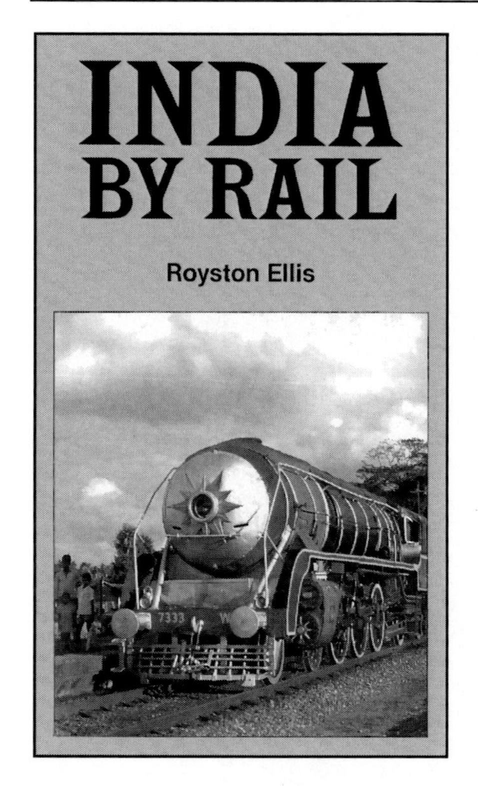

Left: Royston Ellis's railway guide.
Right: The author, sketched by train driver B.S Gill; on the Kalka/Shimla railway.

similar material with a band called the Silver Beetles, who meant absolutely nothing to us as we had never heard of them. But the gig did take place, for there was a one-line report in the *Record Mirror* about a month later, and I am reliably informed that Royston got on rather well with John Lennon.

Strangely enough, that was not the only time that I encountered the work of Mr Ellis. The name was just logged away in the dark recesses of my memory until some thirty or so years later. As it happened, Anna and I were travelling around Southern India by train, and during our stop in Trivandrum we visited a local bookshop and were pleased to find a guide to the Indian railways published by a UK company. But we were even more surprised to discover that the author of this extremely detailed work was the same Royston Ellis, who was apparently now living in Sri Lanka. Inside the cover was a sketch portrait of the author that depicted a balding, middle-aged man with a beard not dissimilar to mine. The brief notes stated that he was *'a poet, pop biographer and youth chronicler before leaving England, at the age of twenty, for a life of travel.'* Well, well, it is a small world, isn't it?

Not too long after that Harrods gig, Jim parted company with Neil Christian. I am unaware of the exact circumstances, but I don't think it was an acrimonious event. Both he and I were moving on to another stage in our lives.

PART TWO

BRIAN, MICK, KEITH AND THE BLUES

I

It proved too difficult to accurately integrate the events described in the previous section with those that involved Brian Jones, Mick Jagger and Keith Richards (or Richard, as he still was in those days). The timescale is in part concurrent, but at a distance of forty-plus years I was unable to recall the exact dates in sufficient detail to overlay them. So, I have deliberately created two separate introductory sections which I trust are more or less in chronological order, and the latter portion of the first section overlaps most, if not all, of this one.

We need to step back to where Jim and I were continuing to try and discover as much hard rock‘n’roll and rhythm & blues as we could unearth. Jim’s prime interest was the unusual instrumental sounds that these records often relied on, while I gradually became more aware of the content of the songs and the accompaniment eventually became a less dominant element. I had started to listen more and more to the slow-tempo ‘B’ sides and began to find them more interesting than the frantic rockers that initially ensured our purchase of these recordings. Certainly Chuck Berry’s ‘Wee Wee Hours’ was an early and lasting influence, as was a London American EP (an extended play seven-inch 45 rpm disc with four tracks and a glossy sleeve with evocative artwork) by Howlin’ Wolf which included the magical ‘Smokestack Lightnin’’. I could not always understand the lyrics, but whatever these guys were singing about was irresistible.

The subject matter in these songs was not the teenage hand-holding romance that seemed to be the foundation for most rock‘n’roll numbers. These artists with their strange names were not seeking romance; they were talking about *sex* and, being of an impressionable age, it all fell on very receptive ears. Daydreams of young girls with blonde ponytails and blue jeans were quickly replaced by implanted images of big-leg women stacked at the back in tight dresses. The use of metaphoric phrases and *double entendres* were a particularly attractive discovery for us and, while we were pretty naïve, we were readily receptive to the use of the automobile as a sexually expressive vehicle. As randy young men we were more than anxious to try and *'look up under the hood and check out the carburettor'*. It surely doesn't take too much imagination to understand our enjoyment of lines like *'She walks like she's got oil wells in her back yard'* or *'You've got river hips, mama, let me bathe in your stream'*. All this imagery, coupled with the intense feeling that the artists injected into the songs, appealed in a way that was very different to anything I had experienced before. This was almost certainly the beginning of my life-long love affair with the blues.

The next step in our education was discovering a specialist magazine named *Jazz Journal*. For us, this was a relatively expensive purchase that was primarily aimed at serious jazz enthusiasts with either modern or traditional tastes. It is fair to say that jazz had very little appeal to Jim or myself at that time in our lives. I think I regarded it as music of the mind, rather than the intestines, and I am afraid I dismissed it as being far too intellectual for my more basic tastes.

However, the magazine did grudgingly acknowledge the blues and at the back of each publication was a full-page advert for Dave Carey's Jazz Shop at Streatham in South London, which was not too far away by train. I thought it would be worth a visit and I went there one Saturday afternoon. It turned out to be a rewarding trip, for there, in amongst rack upon rack of albums by sophisticated saxophonists and cocktail hour pianists, were a handful of blues records mainly on imported American labels. One of these albums had a picture of a very sexy-looking black lady sitting on a bar stool wearing a red sweater and a black skirt, both of which were probably two sizes too small for her. I suspect it was a mixture of lust and curiosity that prompted me to ask the guy behind the counter to play a little of the first track.

It was almost the same reaction to discovering 'Watch Your Step', for again it was only thirty seconds into 'Dust My Broom' by Elmore James & His Broomdusters before I knew I could not leave the shop without this record, as it was surely what I had been subconsciously searching for. I might not have thought so at the time, but it was probably akin to a religious awakening. Without putting too much emphasis on the event, I have probably never recovered from that afternoon. These days, anyone can readily access exciting music of their choice with comparative ease, but back then it was very different.

Many years later, I was fortunate enough to meet Joe Bihari, the man responsible for producing this amazing recording, and I thanked him profusely.

In a strange way, I guess we had an advantage over the modern-day listener. We had so little of this new alien music available to us, that the few records we could find were played over and over again, and we eventually absorbed every nuance. Back in the Fifties, successful recordings remained in the American rhythm & blues charts for months on end. These days, we are bombarded with so-called blues and r&b from all directions, and the quantity is such that I am sure that the public do not have the time or inclination to really listen to most of it. Many seem to just enjoy their favourite sounds while driving along the highway, or in the background while they chat to friends. The sheer number of tracks squeezed on to an eighty-minute CD further erodes one's attention. The average person's record collection would probably take weeks, if not months, to listen to just once. Of course, we now have the almost-obligatory video to go with the recordings, and more often than not the visual image completely supersedes any musical talent. It certainly was all very different forty-five years ago.

Those imported records were hellishly expensive by comparison to any available in Britain, and if I wanted more of them, some tough economic decisions had to be made. So I took stock, bit the bullet hard and sold all my rock'n'roll and rockabilly records. I think Jim was the main beneficiary. I am fairly sure he acquired my previously treasured and subsequently very rare Carl Perkins and Roy Hall singles, and I am absolutely certain that I sold him my very-hard-to-find ten-inch *Johnny Burnette & The Rock'n'Roll Trio* album. This record contained their revolutionary version of the old Tiny Bradshaw hit, 'The Train Kept A-Rollin'', and anyone who has heard this record and subsequently seen the movie *Blow Up* will instantly recognise where those Yardbirds (with Jim in the line-up) got that hypnotic guitar riff from.

That injection of capital meant that I could visit Carey's shop on a regular basis. It was there that I encountered Mick Sales, who was probably the first person I had met outside our little group in Epsom who understood and shared our fascination for this kind of music. We just started to chat at the counter and must have made a really odd pair, for Mick was as short as I was tall. He had greasy swept-back blond hair and smoked 'roll your own' fags (no, no, not homosexuals, you Yanks – or spliffs, for that was still somewhere in the future). In those days, I addressed anyone new that I met as 'face', which was in fact a term I had picked up from Jim. For some reason Mick was particularly fascinated by this terminology, and he would demand that I use it to introduce him to anyone we met. It was Mick who first discovered that Carey would import records from America if you were prepared to pay the price in advance and wait four or five weeks for the discs to arrive.

The prospect seemed mouth-watering, but we were hampered by almost complete ignorance. What in hell were we going to order? Even though the shop did provide a list of what might be obtained, there was really no guidance available to us, and so we more or less chose blindly. Well, not entirely, for we selected artists whose names we thought sounded like blues singers. Let's face it, Howlin' Wolf and John Lee Hooker were surely not going to be xylophone players in Ivy League suits, were they? One notable exception was Jimmy Reed, for, on the face of it, with a name like that, he could have been a singing cowboy. He wasn't, of course, and he turned out to be one of the most hypnotic and influential bluesmen of his generation...but more of that later.

II

Apart from the highbrow *Jazz Journal*, the music press at the time consisted mainly of tabloid-style newspapers with names like *Disc*, *Record Mirror* and *Melody Maker*. By and large, they concentrated on the popular mainline artists of the day including home-grown heroes such as Tommy Steele and Cliff Richard. There was little or no coverage of the sort of artist we would be interested in. Even someone like Chuck Berry would command no more than a few lines for his latest release.

There was also a particularly frustrating development whereby insipid British artists would attempt cover versions of American mainstream r&b crossover hits with totally inappropriate accompaniment. I think perhaps I should immediately qualify this comment in order that there should be no misunderstanding, for I am referring to a period well before the Liverpool group era.

It was one of these soulless Brit transgressions that prompted me to write a very pious letter to the aforementioned periodicals. I think I saw myself as a knight in shining armour riding out to champion the rights of under-appreciated rhythm & blues artists. Perhaps I still do. Anyway, I was shocked and pleased when the letter was actually published, together with my address. I was even more surprised when I received some correspondence from a few other like-minded enthusiasts in other parts of the country. Up until this point, I thought we were indulging our tastes for this kind of music in splendid isolation. Being zealots with a near religious obsession, it was consoling to find others shared our fanaticism.

One letter was from a fellow named Brian Jones in Cheltenham, and another from Graham Ackers in Blackpool. The letters contained little or no personal information and were almost exclusively confined to music matters. However, Brian did write and tell me that he played guitar and informed me of his discoveries and his passion for Elmore James. Graham, who wasn't a musician, did more or less the same. He had the benefit of two other local colleagues, Will Jones and Dave Ward, who shared his interest. In those days, other parts of the country were far more inaccessible than they are now. There were no motorways and, as far as I was concerned, you came from a rich family if your parents owned a car. The national railway system (prior to the Beeching axe) was the main means of transportation for the masses, but it was slow and relatively expensive, so there was little prospect of any of us travelling to meet each other.

However, it wasn't long before Graham made the leap that many Northerners had to undertake and travelled south to find work. He arrived in London to start his first job with a Central London insurance company only a few months after our first correspondence. By then he already had a passion for the amber nectar, with a particular fondness for strong ales, and, as things transpired, it would not be long before he coerced me into trying to keep up with him. I recall we first met for lunch in a West End pub. He was a very warm character and I was taken by his Lancashire directness, which was quite different from the South London stance I was used to. By the time the lunch hour was over, I had consumed far more beer than I could then handle and was not really in a fit state to go back to work. I am afraid it was a steep, winding path from there on.

Of course, I told him about Jim and Brian, and he was also encouraged by the knowledge that there were others who shared our interest. In the next few months, a small but dedicated group of enthusiasts started to communicate with each other on a regular basis. One of these was Mike Ashby, who lived at home with his mother in Tolworth in Surrey.

Graham initially had lodgings in Blackheath (a South-East suburb of London) but eventually, following a few visits to the Ashby household, he became their lodger. I think Mike's mother, Mazie, rather took a fancy to the young Northern lad. Being a lone parent, she was happy to have young people around her in the house and would endlessly make us cups of tea. In return, we had a venue where we could meet regularly to listen to music and exchange opinions. This is when tape recordings started to rapidly expand our group knowledge as we shared the music around our tight circle. I think this is also about the time when Brian and I started to exchange worn five-inch tape spools whenever possible. It is difficult for me to put a date on this period, but I think all this activity took place in late 1961 and early 1962.

III

I know that the small group had been meeting at Tolworth on a regular basis for some time when I got a letter from Brian in the early spring of 1962, which was instrumental in bringing us all together. I already knew that he was an aspiring musician, but I was even more impressed when he wrote to me from 23 Christchurch Road, Cheltenham to inform me that he had met and jammed with someone called Alexis Korner, whose apparent intention was to start a 'proper' rhythm & blues club in Ealing in West London. Brian told me he was travelling up from the West Country for the opening night, and hoped to sit in and play with Korner. Could this really be happening, or was I just dreaming?

Of course, I immediately informed Graham whose reaction was very matter-of-fact. He smiled smugly as he produced a tiny cutting from the *Small Ads* section of one of the music papers that announced the proposed gig. As unbelievable as it might have seemed six months earlier, *our* sort of music was actually going to be played by someone in this country.

So, on a Saturday night in late March 1962, Graham and I set off on the tube for Ealing Broadway with Anna in tow. A few hundred yards east of the underground station on the left hand side of the main street were the already-established premises of the Ealing Jazz Club. In retrospect, it was nothing more than a small dingy basement with a tiny bar at the bottom of the steps, but nevertheless on that night it became Britain's first rhythm & blues club.

23, Christchurch Road.
Cheltenham, Glos.
30.3.62.

Dear Dave,
I was very pleased to receive your letter this morning. I would very much like to meet you. Can you make it to Ealing Broadway R + B club (opp Ealing Broadway Tube Station) tomorrow night? The session starts at 7.30 p.m. I expect you read Jack Good's write-up of the club in the "Disc".

I shall be playing a few numbers there, + would like to introduce you to Alexis Korner, who is a great friend of mine.

The charge is only 5/-, which includes membership for a year. Hope you can make it tomorrow (Saturday).

Yours faithfully, Brian Jones.

It is a guess on my part, but I reckon there were less than a hundred people in attendance. Even so, the room seemed very crowded. Just inside the entrance two girls in low-cut dresses spent the whole evening dancing together. Inevitably, they proved to be far more interesting than the individual who touted raffle tickets for a prize draw that took place at the bar during the interval – although I distinctly remember that the prize was one of the few genuine r&b records actually available in this country, a Wynonie Harris EP that included the song 'Bloodshot Eyes'. Yes, somehow it was still all 'stiff upper lip' and very British.

To be honest, I don't recall being very impressed by any of the performances that night, but the mere fact that our music was being played was in itself a significant enough event in my mind. The wild-haired Korner looked and sounded like an eccentric university academic as he attempted to sing some standard Chicago songs in front of a ramshackle band. The group included the equally incongruous Dick Heckstall-Smith on tenor sax. He was probably a jazz musician by extraction and didn't really do anything wrong, but sounded rather bland and timid by comparison to the hard-rocking tenor soloists we had become used to on those American recordings. Although Korner had a genuine affection for the music he was, quite frankly, a bloody awful singer. He had a classic public school accent and every song sounded like an Oxbridge revue parody. But overall it didn't matter, for we were among like-minded souls, and at least they were trying to play electric blues.

Various individuals were invited to try their luck with the core group. One of these was a podgy, balding, red-faced and semi-pissed Cyril Davies who sang some Big Bill Broonzy numbers and played harmonica much in the manner of his idol Sonny Terry. In truth, he fared little better than Korner, but he clearly had a feel for the music that Alexis could not convey and somehow that endeared him to us. Actually, he looked like somebody's dad, but, what the hell, for our fathers would not be doing this sort of thing on a Saturday night. It is ironic that forty years later every town in Britain now seems to have at least one pub where middle-aged men try to be a weekend Muddy Waters.

Later that evening, a young blond-haired lad joined the group, and to our instant joy he started playing bottleneck guitar in a rough approximation of Elmore James. It transpired that 'Dust My Broom' was the only number that he knew at the time, but it did serve to identify Brian Jones for me and we met for the first time as soon as he left the stage. He was just an ordinary-looking, well-groomed youth who proved to be just as enthusiastic about this music as we were.

In fact, music seemed to be the sole topic of conversation for everyone in that tiny room. During a break, we met a tall, spotty-faced young man at the bar who was expounding on the virtues of T-Bone Walker and Memphis Slim in a very cultured university accent. When the music restarted he eventually got up to sing a number or two with the band. Although he was introduced as P.P. Jones, he would subsequently revert to his real first name, Paul, and develop a successful career with Manfred Mann. Many years later, he would go on to host a British radio programme devoted entirely to the blues, but back in 1962 that would have seemed as unlikely as a man landing on the moon.

In those first few months, we attended the club on a regular basis, but neither Graham nor I can remember whether Mick and Keith were there that first night. However, I can recall them sitting in with Korner's band for a song or two in the ensuing weeks. I think they first approached Brian, who in turn introduced us to them. I quickly established a rapport with Keith as he was a rabid Chuck Berry fanatic like myself, and the fact that I had managed to acquire some Berry recordings from the States that he had not yet heard was all that was necessary to initialise the friendship. Jim's battered tape recorder was put to good use yet again. Mick had a particular affection for Bo Diddley and that went down very well with Graham. But at that time we simply regarded him as just another enthusiastic singer who got up to perform an occasional number with the band – I mean, he didn't even play guitar.

You might wonder what our first impressions were of these soon–to-be-famous individuals, but apart from our shared fascination with the music, we didn't think there was anything special about any of them. Brian was still commuting from Cheltenham for the gigs, Mick was ending sixth form studies and preparing for the LSE, and Keith had a part-time job as a postman. They didn't come from privileged backgrounds and, just like us, they had no money to speak of. Back in those pre-Beatles days we all had regular haircuts, so they didn't look any different from any other teenager you might meet in the street. They were just regular guys. Give or take a few hundred million dollars, perhaps a couple of them still are.

As the weeks passed, Mick and Keith aligned themselves with Brian and regularly performed numbers with Korner's group. Initially, the songs they performed were Chuck Berry and Bo Diddley numbers that were popular with all three of them. They consciously avoided the relatively better-known songs and concentrated on 'B' sides like 'Around And Around', but even so they were still rather frowned upon by the more traditionally-minded Korner.

Brian had reached the stage where he was so obsessed with the fade-out solo in Elmore's 'Dust My Broom' that he would try and play it at the beginning, middle and end of almost any number they performed, if he was given half a chance. Keith continually complained that Alexis's band had no drive and became sensitive to the feeling that Korner didn't really approve of what they were doing anyway. It didn't seem to matter too much to Graham and myself, for it was all very rough-and-ready stuff at the best of times and would not have stood up to very much sober listening in daylight hours. Not that we ever did much sober listening in those days.

It didn't take very long for a strong bond to develop between Mick, Keith and Brian. They had a common goal to form their own working group and it wasn't very long before a name for the band had been decided upon. By now we had all heard that famous Muddy Waters song and I am sure the choice was unanimous. Brian was convinced that they needed to have material that was not being performed by anyone else in Britain, and this is probably the appropriate place to give some credit to a couple of Frenchmen who indirectly influenced the development of this soon to be famous little group.

After reading so far, you could be forgiven for thinking that it was the British who were the first in Europe to discover post-war electric blues, but that would not be strictly correct, for in some ways we lagged behind our Continental neighbours. This situation was exemplified by a series of articles published in *Jazz Journal* in 1960 by the groundbreaking French enthusiasts Jacques Demetre and Marcel Chauvard entitled *The Land of the Blues*. These were borrowed and translated from articles in a French publication called *Jazz Hot* which told of their trip to America in the late Fifties to unearth the then-virtually unknown urban electric blues that was being performed in black neighborhoods in the Northern industrial cities.

These two guys spoke little or no English, yet they were prepared to go into the black urban ghettos where almost no white Americans would dare to venture. It seemed that white Americans were completely oblivious to what took place on just the other side of the tracks in their cities. As Elmore James died shortly after their trip, they were probably the only two white men with any real knowledge of the music to ever see him perform live, and they were almost certainly the first white

critics ever to enthuse about B.B. King. No doubt their subsequent reporting back in France was a major reason why there were more recordings of new electric blues available there than here in England.

Having read these articles, Graham and I somehow learnt of contacts in Paris and Holland that would supply us with records by mail order. I am not sure which of us first imported the disc but a twelve-inch compilation album of Vee-Jay recordings entitled *Bluesville Chicago* was the record that really captured all our imaginations. There were five featured artists, but it was the tracks by Eddie Taylor and Billy Boy (Arnold) that appealed to us most.

When Mick, Keith and Brian heard these recordings, it immediately provided them with the songs they were searching for. I think it is safe to say that this one record provided a large proportion of the material for their very first official repertoire. The numbers that took their fancy were Taylor's 'Bad Boy' and 'Ride 'Em On Down', plus Arnold's 'I Wish You Would', 'I Ain't Got You' and maybe also 'Don't Stay Out All Night'. These songs were almost certainly among the first that the three of them ever rehearsed together. The problem was, they didn't have a regular bass player or drummer, and that was a major hurdle. If I recall correctly, Dick Taylor – later with the Pretty Things – was playing drums with Korner part of the time, but he would also occasionally sit in with the lads. But I am getting ahead of myself….

Brian's isolation in Cheltenham did not last for much longer, as he decided to come to London shortly after meeting Mick and Keith. He found lodgings at 23 Brackley Road at Beckenham in Kent, near to where the other two lived. I can remember him coming over to one of our Tuesday night sessions at Mike Ashby's house on the bus, and bringing his girlfriend and a young baby with him. It was a long journey for them, and their entrance may have initially raised a quizzical eyebrow or two, but nothing more.

IV

By this time I had become fed up with travelling to Bromley and felt I needed to look beyond working on a building site. I realised that this type of employment could eventually become my much-desired passport to travel, but I needed to climb the ladder first. I reckoned that I needed to be at a company's head office if I wanted to progress. So, I joined a civil engineering design-and-build contractor with offices in Westminster. The premises I worked at were above the busy market in Strutton Ground just off Victoria Street – just a short bus ride to the West End, where I would eventually find much more music and meet others who shared my tastes.

This new job was as assistant to a senior surveyor named Nick Llewellyn, who was probably aged about thirty and even had a company car. The firm specialised in large concrete structures, and one of my first site visits with Nick was to the construction of a 200 metre-high power station chimney that was nearing completion. We had to ascend on the hoist in the centre of the stack and step out on the platform at the top, and try not to show the workmen that we were absolutely petrified. It was a calm day on the ground, but howling a gale up there, and the chimney would actually sway a couple of metres in the wind. The car we had left parked at the foot looked like a tiny toy. Workmen swung out over the side to make adjustments to equipment as though they were winged insects while we hung on to the scaffold for dear life. It was a severe shock to the nervous system, but, like many more in the future, I somehow managed to survive it.

I enjoyed working for Nick, but one day I had to leave him to sort things out without my assistance. The boss of the drawing office in Strutton Ground found that water was leaking through the ceiling right above his desk and he felt that, as we were surveyors, we were the guys who should locate it and instigate a repair. Nick and I went to investigate the roof and he deduced that the water was coming in somewhere through the dormer window housing which looked directly over the street three floors below. It was a fine day and he had the brilliant idea that we needed some water to flow over the area to see where it would disappear to. As a dutiful Robin to his Batman, I went for a bucket while Nick climbed out the window and stood on the parapet to watch carefully. He said to flush the bucket of water on to the roof, and I of course obliged.

Ultimately, I maintained that the slope of the roof was too steep, but on the other hand I might just have been a tad over-enthusiastic, for the water poured straight over the edge of the roof, over the canopy and down three floors to completely drench a well-dressed elderly lady who was shopping at the market stall below. I heard her scream and jumped back on to the roof out of sight, but there was Nick in full view on the parapet trying to get back in through the window. She went ape and stormed into the office ready to kill. Now, I felt there was little I could say or do to remedy this situation, so I went and hid in the roof tank room until the furore died down. My company prospects did take a bit of a dive that day.

V

From my new place of work, I found I could easily reach the few specialist record shops that existed in the West End. However, we were all desperately short of money. The jobs Graham and I had paid a pittance, Mick must have had some sort of student grant and parental support, Brian had various jobs as a shop assistant which he changed almost every other week, and Keith was still playing at being a postman.

The Mecca for us all was Dobell's Jazz Shop in the Charing Cross Road. Mick was supposedly studying at London School of Economics just around the corner, and we would regularly meet in the shop during lunch breaks on Fridays. We were in search of anything in the way of tough blues, but in the main the counter staff were aloof modern jazz aficionados in striped shirts with button-down collars. They tended to look down their noses if you didn't enquire about Coleman Hawkins or some other tenor saxophonist. Who knows, perhaps I have become rather like them, for we never see ourselves as others see us. They would just about tolerate us scruffy youths, for, very occasionally, we would actually buy something. Below the main shop was a cramped basement that only dealt in second-hand records and this was a place where we could sometimes find rare gems that we could just about afford. Which brings me to perhaps my one contribution to the subsequent works of a band that was still yet to find its destiny.

One day, I walked down those narrow, well-worn steps into the basement, and saw half a dozen American blues forty-fives hanging on the wall behind the counter, suspended by nails through their large centres. You cannot begin to imagine my excitement, for this was akin to discovering a pile of diamonds on the end of your shovel while digging in the garden. Unfortunately, the guy selling them also knew their worth, and the price per item was about five shillings – equivalent to about half a day's wages at the time. Damn the cost, I *had* to have one of these discs! So, I considered them carefully and chose a blue and silver Chess record (number 1596) by Muddy Waters and his Guitar. I only owned US Chess recordings by one other artist at the time, and that was by Chuck Berry. I already had a few recordings by Muddy Waters, but they were all European issues. This seemed a real find.

I took the disc home and played it and, in all honesty, the two songs must have been among the least inspired that Muddy ever recorded. One was the incredibly monotonous 'My Eyes (Keep Me In Trouble)', the other a rather ordinary melodic piece written by Willie Dixon called 'I Want To Be Loved'.

Despite my reservations, this was indeed a rare discovery and none of the others in our circle had ever heard these numbers before. So, true to our code, it was taped for anyone who was interested. Brian was constantly after extracts from my Jimmy Reed collection and, when taping an album for him, I added the two sides of the precious single at the end of the reel. Well, Brian must have seen something in that Dixon song which has always passed me by, for 'I Want To Be Loved' eventually became the 'B' side of the Stones' first-ever single for Decca.

Strangely enough, Graham also unwittingly made a similar contribution. He was the one amongst us with a real passion for gospel music. Sure, I liked the sound of it, but all those earnest songs of praise were rather wasted on me. I was far more interested in songs about Eldorado Cadillacs and drug store women. However, Graham would always chance his arm on those obscure groups with names like the

102, Edith Grove,
London S.W.10.

Dear Dave,

Herewith the tape on which you very kindly agreed to stick some Reed gear. I couldn't put the blank side on the outside, as I didn't have a spare reel. The one side has Bo Diddley on most of it, – it is an Extra Play tape, so you should easily be able to stick "Rockin' with Reed", "I Can't Hold Out" and flip (Elmore) and your Reed singles (only ones which aren't duplicated on LPs) on it.

Also, Dave, if you possibly could grab hold of one, could you tape "Just Jimmy", the latest Reed L.P. over Bo Diddley. But please don't record over Bo unless it is "Just Jimmy".

This is really very good of you mate – if there's anything we can do for you – let us know.

Cheers,

Brian Jones.

P.S. Was it you who wrote to "Disc" some time ago about R+B and mentioning the Savages + us? We never saw it, but we were talking to Ricky Fensen and Carlo Little the other night and they told us about it. We can't think who can have wrote it. Incidentally, Carlo and Rick should be doing quite a few dates with us in the near future. We can do with a solid rockin' rhythm section!

Hope you had a good Christmas.

Five Blind Boys and the Swan Silvertones. I am sure he just loved all that frenzied screaming, for he is a religious apathetic, just as I am.

It was Graham who discovered the first Vee-Jay Staple Singers album entitled *Uncloudy Day*, which he again obtained from France. When he played the disc to us at Mike Ashby's, we were all immediately impressed, for this was nothing like any other gospel record we had previously heard. The harmonies were very blues-influenced and young Mavis Staples's voice sent shivers down the spine – but most unusual of all was the amazing downhome vibrato guitar of her father and group leader, Roebuck 'Pops' Staples.

Graham soon found that they were indeed a very successful group in America, so he imported their third album, *Swing Low*, and it was eventually taped for the guys like others before. This event only has one noteworthy fact which may be of some interest to you, and that is the last song on the second side of the album. The title and hook line are: *'This may be the last time, may be the last time, I don't know.'* Now, I wonder where you may have heard that before? Anyway, let's jump back to those Dobell's days with one of my favorite little stories from the period.

One Friday Mick arrived at the shop a little breathless and said he had been delayed because he needed a leak after his morning lecture. Whilst in the toilet, he had heard a guy whistling a Jimmy Reed tune in the next cubicle. In those days Reed was our main man and we thought that everything he did was fantastic. Therefore anyone who knew about him was clearly worth knowing.

Unfortunately, Mick took too long to finish his urgent call of nature and, by the time he had stuck his head around the corner of the cubicle, the occupant had left. This incident certainly sums up our attitude at the time, but it also does raise a smile when one considers the possible implications. It might have been quite 'interesting' to have our future multi-millionaire Sir Mick explain how he chatted up some stranger in a public convenience with a line like 'What is that song you were whistling?' The red-top tabloid dailies would probably have paid a fortune for the photo opportunity!

VI

This all took place back in the summer of 1962. However, Dobell's was not our only regular meeting place, for Brian had found a job just a few hundred yards south in the basement record department of a stationers/book shop at the West End of the Strand which I am almost sure was W.H. Smith & Son's. Somehow, he had reached the position where he could actually order records on behalf of the shop. This now seems quite incredible for, while I liked Brian immensely, he was one of the most untrustworthy characters I have ever encountered.

I guess I can hardly take the moral high ground, for I would go down to see him and pose as a customer and let him use a bogus name to order some obscure record we liked the look of in the listings. It might now seem like heresy, but Brian had found a source of Crown records, a cheap label principally sold in American drug stores, and had obtained a few albums by B.B. King. To my everlasting shame, both he and I were initially disappointed to find that his music was relatively sophisticated with big band accompaniment. Where was the slide guitar and harmonica? We had a very narrow view of what we thought was *real blues* in those days, but, to our credit, we did learn fast.

It seems almost unnecessary to say it, but Brian didn't last long at that shop. The stock of unsaleable items he left behind must have been substantial. He might have even tried to avoid the consequences of his indulgent activities by being transferred to another branch, for I remember having to leg it right down to the far eastern end of the Strand to where he briefly undertook the same role in another W.H. Smith store at the south end of the Kingsway.

Graham has similar tales to tell of Brian's less than straight-and-narrow ways. Apparently, he was at his desk in the open plan office at the insurance company where he worked and the phone rang. On the other end of the line was an irate Dutchman by the name of Ellinkhuizen. He had somehow got hold of Graham's work number and was enquiring if it was he who had purchased records from his mail order company in Holland. Graham confirmed that he had and was then asked if he knew someone called Brian Jones. Graham was always an honest fellow and as a result Ellinkhuizen blurted out the sad story.

Graham had apparently given Brian the contact address for the Dutchman and young Mr Jones had ordered a number of expensive imported albums. Unfortunately, the naïve and trusting Ellinkhuizen had dispatched them before receiving payment, and was now desperately trying to recover his losses. If Brian's past record were anything to go by, he had absolutely no chance of ever being paid. By now, Graham had learnt to be philosophical about such matters, but he was going to have to find another record exporter.

VII

It was sometime during the summer that Mick, Keith and Brian got together and moved into a flat at 102 Edith Grove. This was a couple of streets west of where Graham now lived in Hollywood Road, a turning off the Fulham Road just a few hundred yards east of Chelsea's football ground. Graham's place was a huge first floor flat which he shared with three other guys who rented it from a West End actor named Donald Eccles. His flatmates nearly always went home to their parents for the weekends (probably for home cooking with laundry service), while Graham was left in sole charge.

I confess Anna and I did rather take advantage of his good nature and became his permanent weekend house guests. He was very tolerant of our intrusion, but did get a trifle uppity when, in a rather excessive period of Sunday afternoon passion, we broke the leg of one of the beds. Of course, it was not Graham's resting place, so he had to explain the fracture to one of his returning flatmates. In my defence, I claimed that the fault lay with the proximity of the nearest pub. Graham's local, The Hollywood, was indeed very local – in fact, exactly opposite across the street, less than twenty yards from the front door. I am sure Graham and I contributed greatly to the landlord's profits during this period.

Those wonderful weekends would start in the basement social club at Graham's place of work in the West End, where the subsidised booze prices suited our pockets. Near closing time, we would decamp back to Earls Court on the tube for a last beer in the pub before invading the flat for lost weekends. Perhaps 'decamp' is not exactly a tactful phrase, for I recall to Graham's acute embarrassment the night he urgently needed a leak on the way home. He managed to last out the tube

September 1962, possibly in Dave Godin's flat in Bexleyheath, London.
Left to right: Brian Jones, unidentified, Mick Jagger looking very pleased with his picture of Chuck Berry, Graham Ackers, Keith Richards holding another picture of Chuck, and Harry Simmonds, who later managed blues-rock band Savoy Brown fronted by his brother Kim.

journey and raced up the station steps onto the Earls Court Road, and rushed into the toilet of the first pub he could find. He emerged red-faced a few minutes later, for apparently the boozer was a gay hang-out and five interested gentlemen had accompanied him into the toilet. He escaped tactfully, but was more careful in the future.

Because of its location and size the flat became our command centre, and over the next few years all sorts of people would frequent it. These included Mike Leadbitter (co-founder of *Blues Unlimited* magazine), Charles Radcliffe (the left-wing writer and friend of Eric Clapton) and Richard Newall (the Canadian harmonica player later known as King Biscuit Boy), but more of them later.

Naturally, The Hollywood was not the only pub in the area we frequented. Down at the end of the street over the junction with the Fulham Road was the Weatherby Arms. It was a busy place where you could bump into all sorts of local people – including three hopeful but destitute young musicians.

Brian, Mick and Keith were certainly living in near poverty in that hovel round the corner in Edith Grove and they really had no gigs to generate income. I had continued to occasionally meet little Mick Sales at Streatham and introduced him to the three aspiring musicians. I believe it was he who managed to get them that notorious gig at Rosehill at the bottom of Sutton High Street in South London. It was in the back room of a pub on the left hand side of the road called The Bunch of Grapes, and I am sure it was the first time they tried to perform together outside the environment of the Korner band.

When I turned up that evening, I found the back room almost deserted. I don't think they could find a drummer to play with them, though Dick Taylor may have turned up later. It was all a bit of a shambles, as there could not have been more than a dozen people in attendance and most of them hadn't paid to get in. It all degenerated into nothing more than a rough rehearsal, for the gig never really got started in the first place. However, just across the road a few streets further up the hill was the Red Lion, and a couple of months later the boys would play there with a little more success.

If my approximate timescale calculations are correct, this has brought us to the autumn of 1962 and the event which has prompted all this scribbling on my part.

PART THREE

ALL OF US AND THE FIRST AMERICAN FOLK-BLUES FESTIVAL

I

It must have been around early September 1962 when the news filtered down the grapevine. I would guess that it was Graham's old Blackpool buddy, David Ward, in his first few weeks back at university in Manchester, who learnt of the impending performance at the Free Trade Hall. He would have contacted Graham, who was now resident down South, and thus the news went around our little group that the Messiahs were coming. We could hardly believe that *real blues artists* were going to appear here in our country. We were aware that Muddy Waters had toured with Chris Barber some four or five years earlier, but that was before our time. When we learnt of the list of impressive names due to appear, one stood out from all the others: John Lee Hooker. Hooker, Jimmy Reed and Howlin' Wolf were regarded somewhat like mystic gods within our circle, and I can think of nothing that would have been expected with more anticipation.

Graham was the guy with the contacts in Manchester and he was the only one amongst us who actually possessed a driving licence. So, it naturally fell to him to make arrangements. It was he who hired the van for the weekend and made the initial cost calculations for us to consider. The share of the expense split between us would seem inconsequential these days, but back then we were all strapped for cash. It all seems quite ridiculous now, given that Mick is probably the world's wealthiest rock star. Anyway, whatever the cost was going to be, we just *had* to go.

I informed Jim of the momentous news, and initially he was just as enthusiastic as everyone else. However, it wasn't long before he realised that he would not be able to make the journey with us as he was already booked to play a gig with Neil Christian on the Saturday night in London. Despite this initial setback, all was not lost, for we realised that the performance in Manchester was not until the Sunday evening. It was agreed that Jim would travel up by train on the Sunday afternoon to meet us at the venue, and we would find space for him in the van for the journey back overnight. Although he may have been the youngest of the group, he was already earning quite good money from music and was probably better able to meet the cost than any of us.

I can distinctly remember it being a cold Saturday morning on 20 October 1962, but that was not the real reason why I chose to wear a recently purchased black polo neck sweater. In those days polo neck sweaters were *de rigeur* and almost obligatory for any young man with aspirations to impress. In order to look the part, I would have probably worn one even if it had been a boiling hot summer's day.

I took the early morning bus from the bottom of Miles Road to the first pick-up point at the Toby Jug pub at Tolworth on the A3 main road into London. I only mention the exact location because, ironically, in a few years' time, at the height of Britain's first blues boom, Muddy Waters and his band would perform in the back room of this very pub that was less than a mile from Mike Ashby's house. On that October day such an event would not have entered our wildest dreams, but it does illustrate how quickly circumstances were going to change.

Will Jones was already waiting in the pub car park when I arrived and looked suitably frozen. Fortunately, Graham is seldom late and he pulled up bang on time in the white van. Will and I quickly realised that this vehicle had no side or rear windows and only bench seats along the sides. It was the kind of van that ordinarily carried goods or took labourers to building sites. The two of us made an executive decision on behalf of the others and piled onto the front bench seat along side Graham. 'First come, first served' was the law of the student jungle – and as for seat belts, they had not even been invented.

Graham drove up the main road into the city. Our next pick-up was Jeremy 'Jess' Pender, another of the South London circle. He must have been of a very nervous disposition, for it seemed to us that his hands never stopped shaking. I recall that he developed an almost unhealthy fascination for James Brown and was given to uttering occasional Godfather-like screams for no apparent reason. Indeed, he was an unusual sort of chap at the best of times. We also collected Mick Sales, who arrived clutching a truly amazing object that would become the main topic of conversation for at least the first hundred miles of our journey.

Little Mick had clearly been keeping his latest import from Dave

Carey's a secret from us. He had got his hands on the then brand new, hot-off-the-press Howlin' Wolf 'rocking chair' album. The main reason for bringing it with him was to try and get the sleeve autographed by Willie Dixon, who had composed most of the featured songs. It was a clever idea, and I immediately wished I had thought to do something similar. It would be another twelve months before I would have the chance to push a pen and an album sleeve in front of my heroes. Although Will and I were desperately anxious to examine this coveted article, we resisted, for we were not prepared to risk losing our seats.

Graham was a pretty good driver and soon managed to find his way through Central London to a square somewhere to the north of Oxford Street, where we picked up Mick, Keith and Brian. All three were immediately impressed by Little Mick's prized possession, but the real significance of this event will become clearer later.

Leaving the city, we headed north and I believe it was the first time any of us had actually travelled on a motorway. In fact, I think that the M1 at that time was probably the only motorway in the whole of the country. It had just two lanes in each direction and only reached as far as the Midlands anyway. It might seem strange reading this many years later, but it was a novel experience for us to stop at a service station. The lack of other fast roads made it a long, protracted journey and I recall we briefly took a break in the Derbyshire town of Buxton. It seemed like the backside of nowhere. We didn't eventually arrive in Manchester until late that Saturday afternoon.

II

Our destination was Dave Ward's student flat in Dickenson Road. Dave occupied a part of a large Victorian house, where he had a couple of rooms on the first floor. He was waiting for us to arrive and came downstairs and met us in the driveway. Gingerly, he informed the group that his landlady had been giving him a tough time of late, and that he would not be able to find the space to accommodate all of us. True to our student training and philanthropic code, Will and I pushed ourselves forward, climbed the stairs and quickly dumped our jackets on the only spare bed. Squatters' rights had been established while negotiations continued in the hallway. I'm not absolutely certain of the outcome, but I do think that some of our fellow travellers eventually found a bed at the YMCA. However, I do know that the seriously broke

Mick and Brian (or perhaps it was Keith) opted to sleep in the van that we had parked in the driveway. My goodness, it must have been cold that night, for those vehicle bodies were just fabricated from thin pressed metal sheets with no insulation. Undaunted, all our spirits were lifted by Dave's news that there was to be a party that night at the student halls of residence. Apparently, all we needed to do was take plenty of beer and he was sure he could get us in.

We had a few hours to kill and the obliging Dave put the kettle on for some tea. It was then that little Mick played his trump card and showed him the Howlin' Wolf album. Dave's eyes popped out and he made straight for his record player. We all sat around on the floor of his flat and listened intently to every track. It was the first time any of us, including Mick, Keith and Brian had ever heard 'Little Red Rooster'.

To say we were impressed would be an understatement, but it was not the only title that took our fancy: there was also a previously unheard version of 'Goin' Down Slow' that really captured our imagination. Essentially, it was just a very good slow blues with some tortured guitar from Hubert Sumlin. But it did have an out-of-character introduction and a passage spoken mid-way through by someone who clearly was not Howlin' Wolf. We eventually all agreed that this narrator was indeed Willie Dixon, whom we hoped to see the following evening.

The spoken introduction went something like this: *'Man, you know I done enjoyed things that kings and queens will never have – in fact kings and queens will never get, and they don't even know about. And good times? Mmmm...'*

After a verse sung by Wolf, Dixon continued with: *'Now looka here, I did not say I was a millionaire, but I said I have* ***spent more money*** *than a millionaire. 'Cos if I hada kept all the money that I already spent, I would have been a millionaire a* ***long*** *time ago. And women? Great googlie mooglie!'*

Reading this verbatim, it may now seem like absolute nonsense, but hearing it rendered in Dixon's unique drawl we thought this was the dog's bollocks and spent the next two days mumbling *'I did not say I was a millionaire'* at every opportunity. People must have thought we were out of our minds, and I suppose they had a point. When I reminded Dave Ward about it forty years later, he recalled that we played the album non-stop until his landlady complained.

The evening arrived and we were directed to the local off-licence to stock up on beer. In those days everyone drank bitter, as lager was for girls, poofs and foreigners. Bulky seven- or four-pint cans were almost guaranteed to gain you entry to any party. Even if we were down to our last few shillings, we would always, somehow, scrape some money together for beer.

The halls of residence were relatively nearby and as we arrived a fellow student came out of the building and warned Dave that the university had put a ban on residents having parties and guests in their rooms. When he saw our faces drop, he laughed. He then said that we should not worry, as a way had been found around the situation. We climbed the stairs and followed the sound of music to a floor that had a long central corridor with bedrooms on either side. As we entered, we saw that there was a chair or a pillow strategically placed across the inside of the doorway to each bedroom and there were handwritten signs on each door saying *'Residents Only'*. There was hardly anyone actually in any of the rooms, but the corridor was packed and the party was well underway. Clearly, higher education does encourage enterprise and inventive solutions!

I cannot tell you many further details about the party except that we got wasted. The next thing I can remember was waking up around midday in a small bed in Dave's flat. I was still fully clothed with a monster hangover and found a similarly incapacitated, foul-smelling Will Jones next to me, breathing in my ear. We were not a pretty sight.

My head felt like it contained a percussion drill that was trying to break out through my skull. I think Alka-Seltzer had just become a favoured treatment for hangovers in Britain, but I didn't have any with me and just had to slug it out. However, the remembered pain does make me recall an incident that took place in my office around this time.

There must have been some kind of mid-week celebration, for, early one morning, everyone looked a little worse for wear, particularly the little Irishman who ran the accounts department. He was a very likeable guy and I encountered him in the gents' toilet looking very sorry for himself. So I asked him if he would like to try a couple of these new-fangled Alka-Seltzers which were supposed to be a miraculous cure for a throbbing headache. He said he felt awful and would try anything, so I went back to my desk and found some of these new wonder pills. Pre-sealed packages had yet to be invented and in those days they were sold in a glass tube with a screw cap. They were bloody expensive, but I found that after weekends with Graham they were a necessary investment.

I took out two of the coin-sized white pills and gave them to him with a glass of water, but before I could stop him he threw back his head and swallowed one of them whole. 'Oh hell!!!' I cried. 'You're supposed to dissolve them in a glass of water first!' But it was all too late, as he immediately started to look very uncomfortable. Within a minute or two he was being violently sick in the toilet. When this abated, he forced down a black coffee and declared that he felt much better, and that the pills clearly worked. Perhaps it is just as well my father did not encourage me to take up a career in medicine.

But I digress yet again. Eventually the stone-cold contents of the van emerged and together with the other remaining bodies, we congregated in Dave's kitchen where he sheepishly informed us that we had made a hell of a din getting back there the previous night. The landlady had just read him the Riot Act and we had better vacate for a while as he had to do some studying anyway.

III

We had no alternative but to explore the streets of Manchester. Hardly inviting at the best of times, in the winter months they were cold, grey and unwelcoming – particularly on a Sunday afternoon with nowhere else to go. Will tells me that he ended up in some pub with Jess Pender and can't remember saying more than three words before five o'clock. I do not know what the others got up to, but Mick and I and two others (maybe little Mick was one of them) just walked the streets for a couple of hours like lost souls. One thing that we particularly noticed was that girls would happily walk around the streets with plastic curlers in their piled up hair with their heads wrapped up under a bright scarf. It was no big deal really, but just so

very different from London.

We eventually ended up in a square right in the centre of Manchester at about three in the afternoon with post-beer hunger pains. The only place we could find open was a huge basement Chinese restaurant. It was one of those soulless places with square tables. Each had a grey tablecloth and a solitary bottle of soy sauce. However, it did still have a very cheap set lunch menu that was still on offer even though it was now mid-afternoon. We went in and expertly dragged out the proceedings so that we could spend the whole of the remainder of the afternoon there. Four like minds had no difficulty passing the time, as the sole topic of conversation was the impending show that evening. Were these gods going to sound like their records? Were they going to play our favourite numbers? An eavesdropping waiter would have thought we were aliens from another world, and I guess in some ways we were.

Around five o'clock we made our way to the Free Trade Hall, which seemed absolutely enormous, but in fact wasn't really that big by modern-day standards. Jim had the luxury of a leisurely afternoon train journey from London and I met him at a prearranged time near the box office. We eventually found and bought a programme.

Although the festival became an annual event and subsequent shows had plush glossy brochures with explanatory text and good photographs, this first tour had no such luxuries. The accompanying paperwork that passed for a programme was very modest. Basically it was a two-colour folded sheet with a shot of Helen Humes on the front and tiny photographs of all the artists inside. We all felt that the alleged pictures of Jump Jackson and Willie Dixon didn't look like either of them.

While the show has always been regarded as the first *American Folk-Blues Festival*, the heading on the sheet was *Jazz Unlimited* and a large banner with the same name had been hung in the hall. I later learnt that this was the trading name of the promoter, Paddy McKiernan. Whatever, that which passed for a programme included a

Manchester Free Trade Hall, early '60s (from programme).

single page of brief notes on each artist written by someone named Bill Entwistle, who was described as a *'well known Northern collector'*. The writer was clearly a truthful guy, for in his short synopsis he was brave enough to admit that he knew nothing about Shakey Jake Harris, who was one of the artists appearing. When referring to the absence of his picture he wrote: *'We apologise to him, we honestly just didn't have a photograph.'* In fact, there wasn't any listed running order either, but we didn't care. We were there to see our heroes in the flesh and that was all that mattered.

While the promoter who brought the show to Manchester was Paddy McKiernan, I do feel that it is far more important that I acknowledge those who really made this event possible. We may have been standing in a theatre foyer in Manchester, but the concert was not taking place due to any particular British involvement.

Although at this point in time the French and Germans were arguably more aware of this kind of music than us in Britain, I don't think they had any home-grown bands trying to play rhythm & blues. If they did, we were certainly unaware of them. Obviously, language would have been a barrier for them. Even though we spoke English every day, *we* were having continual difficulty understanding the Delta dialect and Chicago ghetto slang that was such an intrinsic part of the recordings we so treasured. What hope did our Continental colleagues have? If we did have any concerns, they would have been unfounded, because understanding the lingo did not deter the two enterprising German enthusiasts who were instrumental in assembling this first ever European blues package tour. I can give you no better insight into their background than to quote directly from Rob Bowman's excellent booklet notes that accompany the first two volumes of the recently-issued *American Folk-Blues Festival* DVDs:

> Horst Lippmann's story is one that could easily been written for the silver screen. Born 17 March 1927 in Eisenach, Germany, Lippmann's father was Jewish and converted to Christianity so he could marry his Christian girlfriend. According to Nazi doctrine, this made Lippmann half-Jewish and potentially put him and his family in grave danger once the Nazi pogroms began in the late 1930s. Fortunately, the Nazis never discovered Lippmann's family background. Nonetheless, by September 1944 Lippmann found himself in trouble with the Gestapo.
>
> Sometime before Horst's tenth birthday, his father had brought a handful of jazz records from the United States. Excited by what he

heard, over the next several years Lippmann collected jazz recordings and availed himself of whatever scant information on jazz he was able to lay his hands on. By his mid-teens, he was publishing on an *ad hoc* basis a jazz newsletter and sending copies to German soldiers on the French front. The only problem was that, as a product of African-American culture, the Nazis had declared jazz a strictly forbidden music.

'Jazz had been strictly prohibited by the Nazis,' Lippman explained to journalist Bill Dahl. 'This newsletter came into the hands of an officer, and then I was imprisoned by the Gestapo.' Lippman was lucky and spent only a handful of days in jail.

During the early 1950s, Lippmann spent his time working in the family hotel business, and it was during this time that he began to promote jazz concerts in Germany. A few months later, he partnered with Norman Granz to bring the now-legendary *Jazz At The Philharmonic* shows to Europe.

In 1955, Lippmann was working the door at a jazz show he was promoting in Frankfurt when a brash young man attempted to talk his way in. The young man explained that he was a broke law student who had just hitchhiked from Heidelberg to see the show. Unswayed, Lippmann turned the man away, who, as it turns out, would be his future business partner, Fritz Rau.

Several months later, with Lippmann being unaware that he had met Rau under such ignominious circumstances, Rau contacted Lippmann about booking a Heidelberg group, the Sound Cave Combo, to play at Lippmann's *Deutsches Jazz Festival*. As he got to know Rau, Lippmann was impressed with the younger man's abilities and asked him to take a job as a road manager for the upcoming 1957 *Jazz At The Philharmonic* tour. Rau leapt at the chance and soon thereafter became a partner in Horst Lippmann Concerts.

In addition to his concert promotion and hotel acclivities, Lippmann was also director of *Jazz Gehört und Gesehen* (*Jazz Heard and Seen*), a bi-monthly television show. Joachim Berendt, known as the 'German Jazz Pope' and author of numerous books on jazz, served as host for this series.

Stopping in Chicago while conducting research for one of his books alongside famed jazz photographer William Claxton, Berendt was invited to a jam session organised in his honour in the garage of drummer Jump Jackson. In Europe at that time there was a general sense that blues was a dead music. For Berendt the jam session at Jump Jackson's was a revelation. Not only was the blues not dead, there was an extremely active, rich, contemporary blues scene in Chicago.

> Berendt returned to Germany and, according to Lippman, enthusiastically proclaimed the blues to be alive and well in America. Berendt also suggested to Lippmann that he direct a show of *Jazz Gehört und Gesehen* featuring a number of Chicago blues performers and/or promote a tour featuring a number of the same blues musicians. Lippmann elected to pursue both options, using the combined revenue from the television show and the concerts to finance the tour and pay the musicians.
>
> With the television production underwriting much of the travel expenses, Lippmann was able to cobble together dates in Germany, Austria, Switzerland, Paris, Scandinavia and, after some struggle, a lone English date in Manchester. While many of his co-promoters had been worried about selling enough tickets to break even, Lippmann was confident that there were enough jazz aficionados interested in the blues to make the shows a success. He was right about the shows being a success, but the audience composition proved to be much different to what Lippmann or anyone else had imagined.

Whoever they imagined might turn up, it probably wasn't us. Nevertheless, I and thousands of other blues enthusiasts thank him and his partner, Fritz Rau, from the bottom of our hearts, for they were instrumental in opening so many eyes and ears. One could argue that what developed later might have done so without their inspirational shows, but no one can deny that they were exceptional groundbreakers.

IV

So, having briefly examined the programme, we searched for and found the other members of our crew. Most importantly we found Dave, for he now had the tickets. The boy had 'done good', for there were two shows and he had got us cheap seats for the first house at six o'clock, but great ones for the second performance which were only a dozen or so rows from the front on the left-hand side facing the stage.

We made our way upstairs to the bar, but by now we were all skint and a long-sipped half of bitter was about all we could afford. The gathering bodies seemed a strange bunch spanning all ages. There had been a folk music following in Britain for some time, and we surmised that those members of the audience with shaggy beards and corduroys had been attracted by the name of the show, which played on the *'Folk-Blues'* aspect. We felt that they would have primarily come to see

THE CAST

JUMP JACKSON FROM NEW ORLEANS, LOUISIANA
Your compere for the evening
—will introduce . . .

HELEN HUMES — FROM LOUISVILLE, KENTUCKY

MEMPHIS SLIM — FROM MEMPHIS, TENNESSEE

"T-BONE" WALKER — FROM LINDEN, TEXAS

JOHN LEE HOOKER — FROM CLARKSVILLE, MISSISSIPPI

SONNY TERRY
and
BROWNIE McGHEE — FROM DURHAM, N. CAROLINA

WILLIE DIXON — FROM VICKSBURG, MISSISSIPPI

JIMMY D
"SHAKY JAKE"
HARRIS — FROM EARL, ARKANSAS

JOE PALIN—from Manchester (U.K.) is tonight's accompanist. A gifted pianist who gave up the piano chair in the Johnny Dankworth Band to return to his business in Manchester. Joe is a well known figure in Northern jazz circles.

Sonny Terry & Brownie McGhee, who were not an unknown quantity. To our way of thinking, the duo sang the sort of singalong blues numbers that the folkies enjoyed. We also suspected that those who were dressed in suits and ties were knowledgeable jazz fans who had come to see the likes of Helen Humes and T-Bone Walker. I am afraid stereotype prejudice prevailed, even in the pre-Stone Age.

The always-ebullient Dave Ward soon herded us into a corner and introduced us to some members of the Northern equivalent of our little blues mafia. The guys who were from Liverpool seemed particularly knowledgeable, but the trouble was I could hardly understand a word they said. It was probably the first time I had ever encountered such strong regional accents. A bell eventually interrupted our earnest discussions and we took our seats.

Possibly due to the sterile atmosphere of the cold hall and our remote seats, the first show did not leave an indelible imprint in my memory banks. However, the second house was a different matter altogether. When we took our places on the floor of the auditorium for the second show, we all sat in a line about a dozen rows from the front. The seats were those horrible brown canvass-covered hollow metal-framed stackable ones that we used to have at school in the Fifties. I guess they typified the austere period we were all about to leave behind.

Unbeknown to us at the time, this event was also something of a landmark in the career of a local lad from Manchester. In years to come Brian Smith would become one of the most prolific photographers of blues artists in Europe, and his pictures would be used by publishers and record companies throughout the world. However, on this grey Sunday in October 1962, he was just nineteen years old and, although he had previously attended many popular music performances, this would be the very first time he would successfully photograph visiting American blues artists.

Press/photo passes may now be an essential requirement for the most modest of gigs, but at the Free Trade Hall there was apparently no need for such formalities in those days. The young snapper merely bought a ticket that gained him access to the auditorium for the second show, and when he left his seat and headed for the stage with his 35 mm Ilford Sportsman, complete with its cheap fold-out flash attachment, nobody objected, not even promoter Paddy McKiernan. His lack of experience must have been apparent, for he received some tips on where to stand and what best to do from a much older and more experienced press photographer who had been sent to cover the show. Brian has always been very grateful for that guidance and has tried several times to discover the man's identity in order to thank him, but without success. In retrospect, Brian will also acknowledge that the additional lighting for the television cameras did help enhance his photos and, as the film taken that evening for the ABC Television arts programme, *Tempo*, seems to have been lost or destroyed long ago, his visual record of what took place that day is the only one that I could find.

Even though I have been aware of Brian's work for a long time, I did not actually contact him until some forty years after the event. I had previously seen his picture of T-Bone Walker at the front of the Free Trade Hall stage in Willie Dixon's biography, *I Am The Blues*, and I am sure the same shot is used as one of the illustrations on display at what is now a museum at the old Chess studios in Chicago.

Brian has been kind enough to let me use those photographs in these pages and, if you employ a strong magnifying glass – or perhaps a microscope would be more appropriate – you will just about see the prominent forehead of yours truly in the audience to the left of the picture. I am afraid you will not be able to recognise any of the more famous faces in the same row for, being six foot five inches tall, I did rather tower above the others, who are obscured from view.

On that night, the stage seemed very high above us and I remember we had to look up at the artists, which I suppose was quite appropriate. It must be said that, in the wisdom of hindsight, these shows took place in the least appropriate circumstances to properly appreciate a blues artist. The atmosphere was utterly sterile and it must have been very intimidating for the performers to face a strange new audience who were white, sober and shackled to their seats. It was all about as removed from a juke joint as one could ever imagine. However, keen anticipation was a strong antidote and the audience was ready to politely applaud at every opportunity.

I cannot recall every detail of the performance, but I will try and convey the aspects that entranced us most. Much heated discussion took place between us in the hours that followed the show, so I have plenty of opinions to refer to.

Clearly, we wanted the sound from the stage to be just like that which emanated from our treasured recordings, and it did not take us long to realise that the sanitised surroundings and echo-laden amplification in the hangar-like hall was going to dash those hopes. Nonetheless, the visual impact was a major compensation.

There was Memphis Slim in his smooth dark suit and slicked back hair with a white streak in the centre of his forehead. He may have had a somewhat florid style of singing and playing piano, but what an impressive figure he looked. At one point during the evening while he was not performing, I spotted him chatting to a long-legged blonde in a leather dress at the side of the stage and their body language was indeed international. My reaction was immediate admiration and envy. Never mind what he sounded like, he certainly knew how to charm tasty women!

The drummer Jump Jackson was hardly a seminal figure in our blues spectrum, but he did a passable job, even if his every rim shot sounded like gunfire in a steel bucket.

The bass player was, of course, Willie Dixon, who was already a legend in our circles. His name invariably appeared in the composer brackets beneath the titles of many of those recordings we so adored. He was an accomplished musician whose enormous stature made his upright string bass seem small, and I reckon if he had ever lost his instrument case he could have used a spare pair of trousers and braces to do the job. He was the 'Mr Fix-it' for the Chess brothers in Chicago and undoubtedly acted as the contact man for many of the artists who appeared in this and subsequent shows. Despite his influential position, he was not a remarkable vocalist and had not made any memorable recordings under his own name. To this day, I cannot readily lay my hand on a single outstanding track by him – certainly not one I could truthfully enthuse about. Of course, blues history is now well aware of his substantial 'behind the scenes' contributions, but back in those far-off days his humorous stuttering rendition of 'Nervous' was his party piece, and it never failed to please the crowd – us included.

Those three were also the backing trio for any other artist who subsequently performed in an ensemble setting, but of course not all of them did. I think it is only right to mention that, while we were young, enthusiastic and very impressionable; we were also pretty immature and ignorant when it came to understanding and appreciating the wider aspects of the blues. We were into small-combo electric Chicago blues in the worst kind of way and almost looked down our noses at other aspects of the music and regarded them as rather *passé*.

There is no doubt that a large proportion of the audience had come to see Sonny Terry & Brownie McGhee, for they were comparatively well known to Europeans, but their folksy country style of performance was just not tough enough for us bloodthirsty hard-nosed blueshounds. The duo had by now shrewdly established exactly what the white audiences would respond to. So, there was plenty of melodic whooping and hollering to delight the majority. We were less impressed, but in retrospect, it has to be said that these two guys did as much as anyone to bring the blues to white ears.

The great Willie Dixon.

We were only marginally more respectful to Helen Humes, who was the sole female singer on the bill. With the possible exception of T-Bone Walker, she was the only jazz-orientated artist in the line up. This now seems an inexcusable mistake on our part. Her mature songs and wonderful delivery were no doubt far too sophisticated for our young ears, but hopefully we have all learnt a little more since then.

One performer who we were very unsure about was Shakey Jake. He may have been an unknown quantity to the programme writer, but we had heard rumours of an incredible single he had cut with the evocatively named Magic Sam on guitar – although at that stage none of us had actually heard the disc. Recently, he had recorded a more readily available album on Prestige that was clearly not in our strict Chicago mould and was viewed by us with some scepticism.

On the night, he turned out to be a straightforward West Side singer who performed well enough within the narrow parameters of our expectations. One aspect of his performance did meet with our unanimous approval. He produced a harmonica and blew as hard as he could directly into the microphone. The man was certainly no Little Walter, but he was the first real bluesman we had ever seen do this and it was exactly the sort of thing we had come to hear. He would unwittingly contribute much to our weekend's enjoyment, but more of that later.

If that had been the full extent of the show, we would have still come away well pleased. We would have at least felt that we had at last been privileged to see real blues artists in the flesh. But there were two artists who would make such an immense impression it is difficult to look back and put their impact in perspective.

By now we had seen the movies *Rock, Rock, Rock* and *Jazz On A Summer's Day* and marvelled at Chuck Berry duck-walking around with his guitar as if it were a theatrical prop, even if in both cases he did little more than strum chords. We had heard that our idols could actually sing the songs we so loved while also accurately playing electric guitar parts as per the record at the same time. Whatever we might have imagined, nothing really prepared us for T-Bone Walker and John Lee Hooker.

T-Bone immediately impressed us without even playing or singing. He was a small, lithe and incredibly dapper man who looked the absolute personification of cool. He not only wore a sharp, light-coloured suit, but also carried his enormous blond, hollow-bodied Gibson electric guitar with its two huge pickups and long lead as

T-Bone Walker. Cool, or what?

though it were a permanent attachment to his body. Whatever pose or position he adopted on stage, it was as if it just went along with him of its own accord.

T-Bone's music was slick, bouncy and sophisticated by comparison to the sort of tough, dirty blues we were heavily into at that time, and, taking that into consideration, it makes it even more amazing how impressed we were by his performance. This guy was just in total control as he swung the guitar out in front of him played it almost

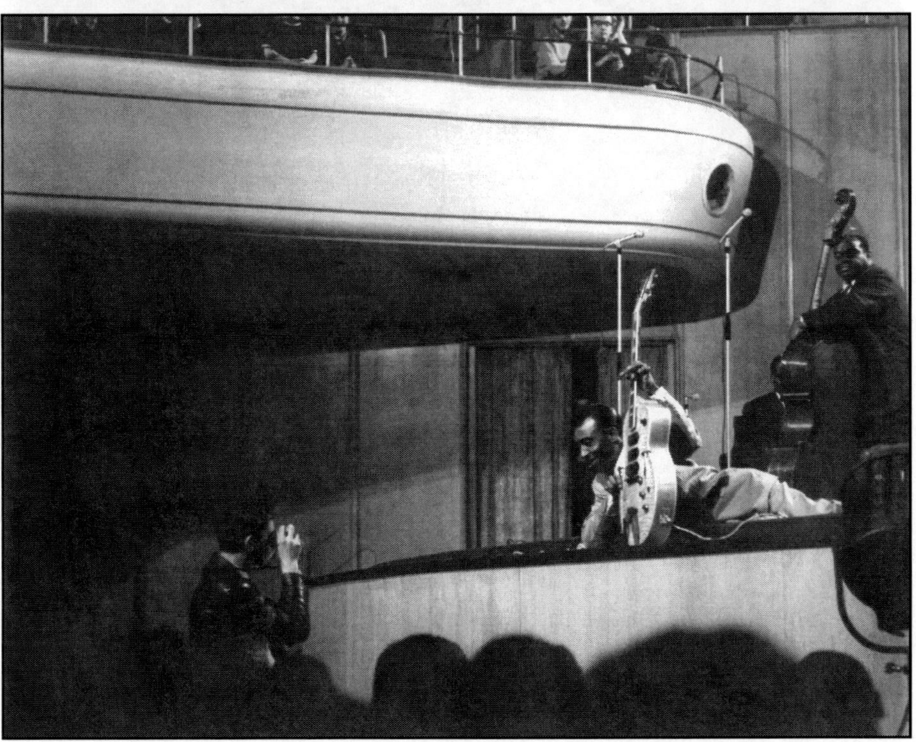

horizontally. We had never seen anything like this, and there he was with all that showmanship right in front of us. I cannot recall the exact numbers he sang, although I do know that he, of course, performed his famous 'Stormy Monday'. His playing seemed effortless, and his set just got better and better as he dropped the guitar between his legs and then swung it up behind his head for a solo. I did not look at Jim, Keith or any of the others while this was all going on, but I can tell you that afterwards they were full of praise and mightily impressed. Half the young males in the world might one day stand in front of a mirror with an imaginary guitar, but not one of them could hope to look as cool as T-Bone appeared that evening.

In a way, it's much easier to give you an idea of what Walker's performance was like and how it affected us, for it was so extreme and extravagant. John Lee Hooker could not have been more different, and his performance and our reaction is far more difficult to overview. He was the only solo act and, if I remember correctly, sang just three numbers without any backing apart from his own guitar. He walked on in a dark grey suit looking very nervous. He too, played a light-coloured Gibson, but it certainly was not the same model as Walker's. One of the things that fascinated us was his stutter. We had heard this on record, but quickly realised was it not affectation, but a normal part of his speech.

Again I'm not sure what numbers he performed, but 'Boogie Chillun' and 'I'm In the Mood' certainly come to mind. I'm not exaggerating if I say that all of us were transfixed, for this was the main man we had come to see. He may have looked urbane in that suit up on the huge stage in a strange environment, but when he started playing and singing we thought that he was the very embodiment of a downhome bluesman. It may have been a damp and grey Manchester outside, but we thought we were sweltering down on the Delta. We were absolutely silent through each number, applauded politely at their conclusion and keenly awaited the next. When it became apparent that his very short set was at an end, we went ape and screamed for more, but to no avail. Anyone who had taken a photograph of the satisfied grins on the faces in that row of seats would indeed have had a memorable picture.

For the finale of the show all the artists gathered on stage to perform an ensemble version of 'Wee Wee Baby', and when the song finally came to an end and the applause died down there was an uncomfortable moment when both the artists and audience paused. It

The one and only John Lee Hooker.

was as though people did not know what to do and were waiting for something to happen.

Something did happen, and we were in the right place at the right time, for, when a few people right at the front climbed up on to the elevated stage to greet their heroes, we immediately decided to join them. It was absolute chaos, and I am certain that it would not be allowed these days. It was every man for himself and I made up my mind that I would get to shake Hooker's hand no matter what. By the time I got near him he looked shell-shocked and one can hardly begin to imagine what this guy must have been thinking. Here he was, a black bluesman who was almost unknown in white circles in his own country, being treated like the messiah by a horde of spotty-faced white youths. I could see that others were getting him to sign the paltry sheets that passed for a programme, and so I decided to do the same. A borrowed ballpoint pen was put to work and John Lee scrawled his name. It would be nice to show you that signed programme now, but some years later it became a desirable item for collectors and I am afraid during a period of weakness and dire financial necessity I sold it at one of Sailor Vernon's notorious auctions. C'est la vie.

Having achieved my initial goal, I extracted myself from the rugby scrum that now surrounded Hooker and looked across the stage. There in the middle were Mick and Brian, who had trapped Shakey Jake in front of the drum kit. (Just imagine it for a moment, here were the Rolling Stones mobbing someone else!) I left them to it and made my way towards other artists, who I also got to sign the programme. It does now seem incredible that this mêlée was allowed to happen, but nevertheless it did.

Eventually, the artists managed to escape and we slowly made our way out of the hall. As we congregated on the steps, group euphoria set it. We were now all anxious to tell each other our opinions of the show. It must have been getting late in the evening but there was no need for us to rush to leave. Public transport would not be starting back in London until about six o'clock the next morning, so to arrive back at the city early would be pointless. We thanked Dave for all his efforts and said goodbye. Graham went to rescue the van from wherever he had parked it, and eventually we piled in and set off South in the early hours of Monday morning.

V

Strangely enough, the trip back to London turned out to be almost as memorable as the show. Under normal circumstances, I would have slept the whole journey, but everyone was on a high and a party atmosphere prevailed. We were all talking at once when suddenly Brian (or maybe it was Mick, I'm not certain) produced a harmonica that had been given to him by Shakey Jake. What a prize! We were all very envious. Then one of them started to play it, and that was the signal for us to start singing. You might feel that downhome blues is not the sort of music to sing along to, but you would be very wrong. We all knew every line of every Jimmy Reed and Muddy Waters song you could name, and the Lancashire night began to echo to the ensemble chorus of 'Baby What You Want Me To Do' and 'Bright Lights, Big City'.

Brian had a wicked sense of humour and he started to parody some of his Ealing club counterparts. He had us in stitches, for, although he greatly admired Alexis Korner, he couldn't help but take the piss out of his public school accent. Try and imagine a vintage BBC newsreader announcing a line from a Muddy Waters blues, *'Oh baby, look how you have got me standing around crying'*, and there you have it. We were just totally helpless.

He was no less sparing with the much-loved Cyril Davies. Let's face it, Cyril did like the bottle and his speech was slurred at the best of times, so he was a natural for those mush-mouthed Jimmy Reed songs. He also had a rural manner of speaking and Brian had him off pat with lines like, *'When eyes sings a Jimmy Reed song, eyes tends to sound like Jimmy Reed'*. This became a blues mafia quote for years after.

The only trouble was that Brian, a complex character at the best of times, was a very nervous passenger. Sure, Graham had his foot down on the pedal and the overloaded van (we had now had to find space for Jimmy as well) was a bit unstable, but it was the middle of the night and there were very few cars on the road. As Graham ploughed on due south, Brian became increasingly agitated about the speed we were travelling and kept asking Graham to slow down. What a waste of breath that was, for Graham never took a blind bit of notice.

Eventually, we made it to the motorway and came across an all-night service station. Again, for most of us this was a real novelty. However, Jim was a seasoned night-traveller by now and he clearly enjoyed talking me through the delights of the fry-up menu. After a feed, we resumed our journey and it was still dark when we reached the outskirts of London. Graham dropped passengers off at various points as we went through the centre of the city. At some point we passed a Circle Line tube station and I got out, waved goodbye, boarded the first available tube and went straight to the office in Victoria. It must have been the one and only time in my life that I ever turned up early for work. On the other hand, I was falling asleep by mid-morning, but I had a big smile on my face.

There is a little postscript story that Graham liked to tell regarding the expense of our trip. Apparently, he worked out the cost of the hire of the van plus the petrol involved and calculated the donation required from each passenger. The sum per person in the pre-decimalisation currency of the day was ten shillings and sixpence. That is just over 50p in present-day money, but it represented quite a lot more in 1962, for I was then earning about £4 a week. However, true to their destitute status, some of our group skilfully avoided payment, and he never did manage to get the money out of Brian, Mick or Keith, who were continually on the scrounge like the rest of us.

Many years later, Graham and I would regularly meet for a beer or two and consider the outstanding debt. We decided that, given that Sir Mick ranks amongst the world's richest men, and Keith must be worth a few bob as well, they could now afford to pay up. It would be nice to think that poor old Brian was still around to shell out too, but sadly that is not the case. Applying reasonable compound interest from 1962, the debt was now quite a bit more than ten shillings and sixpence. So, lads, if you ever get to read this, the next round of beers is definitely on you!

PART FOUR

AFTERMATH

I

1962 soon came to an end, and the following year would see the formation of the first classic Rolling Stones line-up, who would go on to become a part of modern music history.

Inevitably, meeting up with Brian, Mick and Keith became a much more infrequent event. I was now studying at college on a part-time basis and, along with some of the guys in my year, I used to eat at a cheap late-night restaurant in a basement at the north end of the Earls Court Road called the Sou Sol. It was a sure sign of an upward movement in their financial fortunes when, one night, I bumped into Mick and Keith dining there. That would have been unthinkable a few months earlier, as they would have been pushed to afford a sandwich between the two of them. We had a brief conversation, but as they had a couple of girls in tow I kept it to a short and sweet enquiry about how the band was doing.

By this time they had cut their first record and I must be honest and say that I was not particularly impressed, as I thought it to be a rather inferior version of a not particularly inspired Chuck Berry song. It seemed to me that the dreaded studio mafia must have had more than a hand in the sedate arrangement of the number. Of course, the previously mentioned 'I Want To Be Loved' was on the flip side, but, as I have said before, I was not particularly taken by that song either. However, it did get the guys on the road to recognition and I can truthfully say that I was pleased to see them succeed.

In those days I was trying to work, study and burn the candle at both ends simultaneously, and there really wasn't much in the way of spare time in my life. So, it was some months later that Graham and I ventured out to Richmond to see the now-complete band play. Strange as it may seem, it was a surprise for us to find the place packed with new adoring fans. The band's music was very much the same, if perhaps a little more frantic, but their performance and demeanour had become very mannered and I think we left before the end.

In retrospect, I do feel that I should be very grateful to the lads, for there is no doubt that what they were doing was indirectly making the general public aware of the music that we so enjoyed. Eventually, I would benefit enormously. Shortly, the previously unthinkable would happen and we in Britain would soon be able to regularly go out to clubs all over the country to see real American bluesmen perform. The likes of Little Walter, Jimmy Reed, Howlin' Wolf and Sonny Boy Williamson would soon be touring with all sorts of home-grown bands with names derived from every conceivable blues song.

This was still a little way off in the future, but we did gradually discover that there were in fact more people than we initially thought who were listening to this new electric blues.

II

As early as the summer of 1962, a small advertisement appeared in *Jazz Journal* inviting replies from those who would be interested in participating in a proposed Blues Appreciation Society. That did seem to me to be a rather grandiose title. I'm sure we initially felt that perhaps only university professors wearing Harris Tweed jackets need apply. But, undaunted, Graham and I decided to respond and thus became two of the 26 founder members of an organisation that was run from a quaint antique shop in Bexhill-on-Sea in sleepy Sussex. Initially, we received a few typed circulars informing us of the goals of the society. From such humble beginnings the world's very first – and arguably most influential – blues magazine was born.

The more sedate acoustic blues style was already an established part of a white folk music scene that had flourished since the mid-Fifties. However, r&b and blues commercially marketed for black consumption was a virtually unexplored form of music in both Europe and white America. Even though it was on everyone's doorstep in the USA, it was almost totally ignored by the Caucasian population. As a result, blank sheets of paper were ready to be filled with every aspect of this music.

A grand total of seven pages were somehow printed (this was well before the use of photocopiers) and a crudely stapled first issue of *Blues Unlimited* was published in March 1963 at a cost of one shilling and sixpence. It would continue to flourish for some twenty-five years and established a reputation as the premier journal in its field. The publication eventually attracted a worldwide subscription list that even included the likes of Billy Gibbons of Z.Z. Top and Henry Vestine of Canned Heat. In fact, Henry even contributed to the magazine at one stage.

The editor was Simon Napier, the proprietor of that strange antiques shop. Regular writers included Mike Rowe, John Broven and Paul Oliver, all of whom would subsequently write definitive books about the music. However, the driving force behind the venture was the incomparable Mike Leadbitter.

Although Graham and I found something in common with all of those involved with the magazine, in Mike we discovered something special. Although he took the idea of research very seriously, like us, he regarded the music as a vehicle for partying and good times. He was also very partial to the amber nectar and that, of course, automatically endeared him to us. We quickly established a natural bond and would go to visit him in far off Bexhill. He would reciprocate and come to London to party with us.

Bexhill-on-Sea had a vague notoriety, for it was the place where people went to retire peacefully, and it was rumoured to be the town with the oldest population in Britain. Pensioners would move to care homes and spend their last years taking the sea air. Perhaps this obscure statistic goes some way towards explaining why the few young people who lived in Bexhill behaved in the way that they did. Anyone who knew Mike would hardly describe him as the status quo, but by comparison to some of his companions he must have seemed relatively normal.

One of his drinking buddies was a young man named Jesus Pious Waghorn. Yes, ten out of ten for deduction, Mrs Waghorn was rather enthusiastic about the Catholic religion. She even had a picture of 'you know who' on the wall in her toilet. Her son was a plasterer and had a splendid display of long, unkempt red hair (bear in mind that this was 1963, and everyone except perhaps the Beatles was still going to the barber's for a short back and sides). Invariably on a Saturday night, Jesus would tour Bexhill's public houses wearing an ankle-length black robe and a large cross on a chain around his neck. While sinking pints faster than a sailor home from the sea, he would get into mock theological arguments with any customer who cared to partake. Of course, Mike found this all hugely amusing, until one day Jesus went a step too far. He purloined some of Mike's rare and treasured Otis Rush forty-fives and persuaded the local landlord to put them on the pub jukebox. Needless to say, Mike did not think that was quite so funny.

Left to right: Dasher, me, Jesus and Mike in Bexhill.

Dasher was another of Mike's quaffing cronies and his party piece at pub closing time was to be towed around the town on a pair of roller skates at the end of a rope attached to a van. Most of the time nobody seemed to notice, for Bexhill was like a morgue even on Saturday nights.

On Sunday mornings, the guys would recover from their hangovers and continue one-sided arguments with the religious broadcasts on the radio. After a midday visit to the boozer, they were in the habit of taking a little exercise and would crawl along the seafront on all fours snapping at the heels of the passing pensioners like pet dogs.

These activities are not quite those one might associate with serious academic music research, but they were the by-products of our lost weekends. All of this did culminate in one notorious occasion when the more austere Simon Napier invited the esteemed American Folklore Professor, Dr Harry Oster, to visit the headquarters of this now influential magazine. He was a learned gentleman from Louisiana University and had been instrumental in recording Snooks Eaglin for the Folkways label. The good doctor arrived at Sackville Road and Simon ushered him through the shop and down the stairs into his basement where he found us all pissed out of our brains dancing the twist to 'It's You Baby' by Sunnyland Slim.

Unlikely as it might now seem, Mike actually persuaded a touring Texas bluesman, the wonderful Juke Boy Bonner, to visit his seaside home town. He was taken down the pub, of course, and he developed a strong affection for the local ale. The man must have seen something in

Left to right: Jesus, Mike and me. Bexhill again.

the place that we all missed, for he subsequently wrote and recorded a song entitled 'B.U. Blues' about the town and its magazine. Needless to say, the pensioners in their retirement homes remained oblivious.

Mike's achievements were indeed remarkable, for his groundbreaking discoveries enabled us to start to understand the significance of this music in a way that is now rather taken for granted. When his discographies were eventually collected together and published in *Blues Records 1943-66,* he would spend a lot of his time at the offices of the publishers, Hanover Books, just north of Oxford Street in Central London.

By this time I had changed jobs yet again and was working for a construction consultant in nearby Soho Square. Mike would sometimes phone me in the office during the afternoon. He would casually say something like 'I am having a few beers with Homesick James (or whoever was touring at the time) upstairs at the Devonshire Arms. Do you want to come and join us?' I could never resist, and would sneak out on some pretext and try and spend an hour or two in their company without getting completely wasted. I would then have to go back to the office for the last hour of business and endeavour to look busy and sober.

Given all the knowledge that now exists, it must be difficult for those of another generation to comprehend how remote and undiscovered the music was just forty or so years back. Artists that the public now regard in awe were almost completely unknown outside their local black community in those distant days. White America had other things on its mind, and if you had mentioned the word 'Cajun' or 'zydeco' to the average man in the street he probably wouldn't have had a clue what you were talking about. To his lasting credit, Mike

Leadbitter probably did as much to make America and the rest of the world aware of this sort of music as any other single individual.

If you ever get the chance to see it, there is a wonderful little low-budget documentary film called *The Blues According To Lightnin' Hopkins* which was shot in the mid-Sixties by Les Blank. It revolves around Lightnin's home in Houston, Texas, and gives a terrific insight into the artist's way of life. There is only one solitary white person to be seen anywhere throughout the movie. One segment is shot at an all-black rodeo, and there, sitting in the bleachers, where no white American would have even contemplated going, is a chubby chap from Sussex, England. Yes, Mike Leadbitter was a remarkable individual and it was a huge shock and a tragedy for us, and the music world, when he died very suddenly from undiagnosed meningitis at the age of just 32. Much of the music from the Southern states that we have come to enjoy would have remained undiscovered for far longer had it not been for his endeavours.

III

Gradually, awareness and interest in the music increased and the *American Folk-Blues Festival* toured again in 1963. The word was getting around, and it visited more than one British venue. In fact, it became an annual event for a few years and subsequent countrywide tours ensured that many budding blues-rock stars of the future could pick up tips first-hand – although Jimmy Page and the Rolling Stones had beaten them all to it by at least a year.

Although Jim was enjoying this gloriously rich vein of blues activity at the same time as the rest of us, he had plenty of other irons in the fire. To a certain extent he was just biding his time. He severed his relationship with Neil Christian, who later celebrated a modicum of success with a typically manufactured solo hit entitled 'That's Nice'. Again, I was very pleased for him, but it was not the sort of music I could get very enthusiastic about.

Jim was undoubtedly an intelligent lad and I think he took his school studies fairly seriously. Coming from our austere post-war background with the natural expectations of our parents it was not easy to immediately decide on a career in music. It was never regarded as a secure form of employment. I vaguely recall Jim toying with the idea of eventually working in a laboratory, but, like so many young teenagers, he was by no means certain about the direction he wanted to go in.

It wasn't long before he enrolled at the local art school at the bottom of the High Street in Epsom. He was certainly able to appreciate artistic endeavours, but I saw some of his early attempts at drawing and you didn't have to be a serious art critic to see that his real talents lay elsewhere. I don't think he was in the best of health during this period either. He was a pretty pasty string bean of a kid at the best of times, and a period of dabbling in matters other than music was probably exactly what he needed. I was now living away from home most of the time and would only get to see him every now and again at weekends.

It was during this period away from regular band gigs that Jim got into session work. I am afraid I can't tell you how this came about because I just don't know. However, I would regularly go around to his house on Saturday mornings to catch up with the news. He would tell me about his initial problems at the studios, mainly due to his inability to read sheet music. Those in charge were still keen to have him around, despite these apparent shortcomings, because he brought with him new ideas and sounds that were way beyond the older studio professionals.

It was in the studio that he first met Big Jim Sullivan, whom he admired greatly. Although Jim had been influenced by other guitarists in his early years, and had borrowed from them, I think that Sullivan could probably be regarded as his first mentor. Jim certainly revered his work, and his playing was stylistically similar at this stage of his development.

I think he first worked at Decca, and during our chats he would describe to me the sessions he had played on. He was frustrated because he didn't get any real feedback on how things had gone. A brief playback in the studio didn't leave a very lasting impression. Eventually, the recordings would be released commercially and Jim would have to go to the local store and purchase a record in order to hear what his work sounded like. There certainly wasn't much in the way of freebies and promos back in those days. He would play me the records, and occasionally express disappointment when he felt his best efforts had been lost or buried in the mix.

I can't remember all those records now and, anyway – he was only one guitarist amongst several in the studio – but I do know that one of his earliest experiences was playing on 'Diamonds' by Jet Harris & Tony Meehan, which topped the UK charts in February 1963.

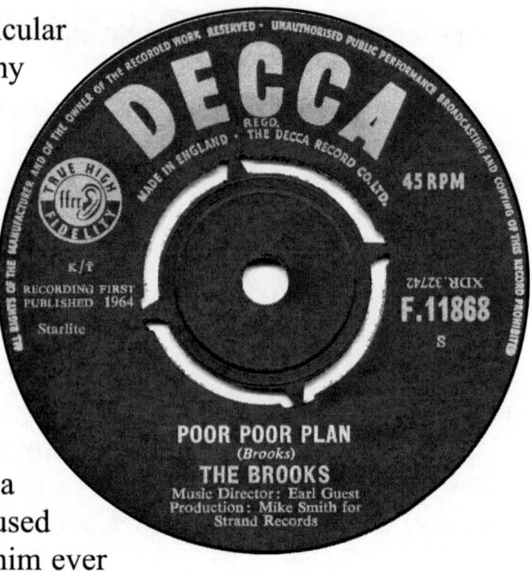

I do clearly recall one particular recording that has stuck in my memory. There was a male duo on Decca, who were called the Brooks and were certainly nothing special. They had earlier made a string of moderately successful records for Pye as the Brook Brothers. Although Jim carried a metal slide in his guitar case (and a glass bottleneck for a short period), he very seldom used it. In fact, I can hardly recall him ever using it, other than fooling around with a blues for me in his front room. Apparently he was in the studio when the two brothers had a session where they were to record a typical teen-appeal 'A' side – a jaunty reworking of the Chimes' 'Once In A While' – and something more uptempo was needed for the flip. The number chosen, 'Poor Poor Plan', was a rather routine rocker that clearly required something to give it a lift. It would seem that the regular sessionmen were lacking inspiration and young Jim the apprentice was given free rein to insert something a little more radical in the instrumental portion. I can remember him proudly producing the disc, and there at the mid-point was a brief slide guitar break. I don't think it was anything really special, but it was distinctive and I think it was a huge boost to his confidence.

Time passed by, and one day he rang me and said he had been approached by Cyril Davies, who was breaking away from Alexis Korner and was about to have his first single release with 'Country Line Special'. Cyril was proposing to use Screaming Lord Sutch's rhythm section for his gigs. These guys were drummer Carlo Little and bassist Ricky Fensten (apparently his real name was Brown). They were well known to Jim and had already been around the block a few times. Jim thought I would enjoy it and took me along one Sunday afternoon to what must have been Cyril's first 'solo' performance without Alexis Korner. It took place at what had previously been Ken Colyer's Jazz Club just off the Charing Cross Road. The band, which included Jim on guitar, had only got about six or seven numbers under their belt and it was almost like a rehearsal in front of an invited audience.

There was one musician in the group who particularly impressed me, the quiet and reserved pianist, Nicky Hopkins. When the band performed a version of the Chuck Berry instrumental, 'Blue Feeling', I was very taken with his keyboard work, which was a pleasant change from all the heated harmonica and borrowed guitar licks. I think Jim's flirtation with the group only lasted a few weeks, although I do vaguely recall a similar evening at the Marquee before he drifted away. I am sure Jim would acknowledge that he was never really a mainstream blues guitarist.

IV

With the regular session work he was now getting, Jim was not short of funds and could afford to sleep in and do far less travelling. However, he certainly did enjoy the blues and wanted to keep up with all the artists that were now starting to visit Britain, but he had commitments that meant he couldn't attend very many of their gigs. With this in mind, we hit upon the idea of making our own pirate recordings.

It might seem strange to readers with minidisc players and mobile phones stuffed in their pockets, but back then the portable cassette tape recorder had still not been invented. Everything we recorded at that time was on reel-to-reel. A five-inch spool was the standard size, although you could get larger spools if you had an expensive, state-of-the-art machine.

Jim was always anxious to keep up with any technical developments and, as I have said, he was already recording himself at home. He had progressed to a point where he was undertaking some crude editing and overdubbing on his new four-track machine in the front room of his house in Miles Road, which was fast becoming like a mini-studio.

Somewhere in the hi-fi shops of Tottenham Court Road in the West End of London, Jim found the first portable tape recorder either of us had ever seen. I guess its dimensions were approximately 12 x 4 x 8 inches and seemed to have the weight of a lead box. It was powered by several large torch batteries, which only added to the load. There were two three-inch spools attached on the top that provided just enough tape for about fifteen minutes recording time.

Jim, mid-'60s.

After some experimentation, we agreed that I would take this contraption to gigs and try to record the artists for posterity. (Actually, not for posterity really, just for Jim and myself.) We didn't give copyright protection a second thought. Maybe we regarded ourselves as musical adventurers and anything that enhanced our knowledge and enjoyment was fair game. It now it seems inconceivable that I carried this bloody thing around to all those venues, for I had no car and did it all by public transport.

I was certainly not short of gigs to attend. For a relatively short period, in Britain we were seriously spoilt by a continuous stream of visiting blues artists. I am afraid I really had little or no interest in the emerging British bands that tried to faithfully copy this music. I am sure my attitude must seem terribly pompous to some of you, but as a ravenous blues enthusiast I could not see the need to spend time and money on imitations when I could just as easily have the real thing. I am sorry if that sounds elitist, but if you could have a Ferrari for the same price as a Ford, which would you choose?

I went everywhere I possibly could to record people: John Lee Hooker at the Flamingo, Jimmy Reed accompanied by John Lee & The Groundhogs at a dancehall in South London, even Chuck Berry on his first-ever visit to England at the Hammersmith Odeon (or at least as much as I could before they brought the fire curtain down to quell the riot that erupted).

How did I get away with it all without being nicked? I guess nobody had given the idea of a pirate recording a second thought back in those days. I even took the wretched machine to the huge Fairfield Halls in Croydon and sat in the balcony with Graham to record some of the annual *American Folk-Blues Festival.*

The main problem with the short tapes was that they would run out in the middle of numbers. I had to scrabble for the half a dozen replacements in my pocket and fit them in as quickly as possible so as not to miss too much. Back at his house in Epsom, Jim would get frustrated and curse at me if I had recorded a good number and somehow the guitar solo was missing. He would edit and splice the tapes together and we would re-record them as more or less complete numbers. The sound quality wasn't too brilliant, but we were just happy to hear more of this music.

Many years later, I dug the tapes out again and transferred some of them to a CD. It was amazing to think that I had preserved the sound of our youth on a little shiny disc, for there were the likes of Little Walter at a pub in Blackheath, and Howlin' Wolf and Jimmy Reed at an old cinema in Guildford. They did eventually come in useful, for somehow the authors of *Blues With A Feeling*, the excellent biography of Little Walter, learnt of my efforts and asked for a copy of my recordings of his gig with the Sheffields for their research.

Remembering that Jimmy Reed gig at the Ricky Tick Club (it was just a fancy name for an old converted cinema probably dreamt up by the promoter, Rik Gunnell) did get me thinking about the circumstances surrounding our visit to that venue. Hopefully you might find them amusing.

V

In 1963 I reached the grand old age of twenty-one, and, as I have already said, my mother had died when I was much younger and so I needed someone to spoil me on my birthday.

It happened that one of my father's sisters had made quite a pile after the war by setting up nursing homes in Bayswater in West London. Her clientele were the aging parents of the rich and famous who could afford to pay her hefty charges. Aunt Hilda was her name and she was quite a character. She was a maiden lady, and I suspect the love of her life was killed in the war. She made pots of money from her nursing home business, but to her credit she knew how to spend it. I certainly remember previous trips to see her when I was well and truly spoilt, but nothing prepared me for my twenty-first birthday.

My father informed me that I had been summoned to London to see her and it would be a good idea if I took along my steady girlfriend, Anna. Apparently, Aunt Hilda wanted to give her the once-over. We dutifully obeyed and went to her palatial house in Porchester Terrace. There, we were summoned to her lounge where she reclined on a huge sofa surrounded by expensive antiques and works of art. It all seemed like a set from an old black & white Hollywood movie. Thankfully, she was rather taken with Anna and gave her a huge stuffed teddy bear as a present. Then she took me aside and said that, as it was a special birthday, I should have a special present. You can try and put yourself in my shoes when my aunt handed me a set of keys and said that she was giving me her Mercedes 190SL sports car for my birthday!

I did know that she was one fast lady with affection for such motors because over the years I had been summoned to her house on previous occasions, just to be driven all of three streets away to Whitley's. This was a swanky department store where Brian Jones had actually worked for a few weeks before he was, as on many other occasions, fired. Name the classic car and at one time or another she would have had it. I can recall the Facel Vega, the Jaguar with the wire wheels and the fancy Volvo like the one Roger Moore used in the old *Saint* TV series. All of them were white. She must have been colour blind because she just loved white.

Anyway, I was told to go downstairs and examine my present, and there it was parked in the street with its drop top down and, of course, it was gleaming white.

You could be forgiven for having some doubts about this little story, but I will swear to anyone it is true. However, you have not yet been presented with the ironic twist to the tale for, you see, I had not yet learnt to drive. Hilda being Hilda hadn't thought for a moment how I was going to pay for the insurance, afford to run the bloody thing or even remove it from outside her house. But how could I be ungrateful? I bounced back down the street to the tube station with Anna, having just received the birthday present to end them all.

I soon came down to earth with a bang. What was I going to do with the damn thing? I phoned Graham, who was the only person I knew who could drive and told him the news. After he picked himself up from the floor, we arranged to meet to collect the vehicle.

Cruising with Graham on Miles Road.

Thankfully my aunt had slipped me a £10 note on the way out for petrol, for the wretched machine guzzled the stuff like a drunken sailor. I reckon we used all the money my aunt gave me just getting the car back to my father's house in Epsom. We had no garage, of course, and it remained parked out in the street where our neighbours could look at it from behind net curtains and consider where I had stolen it from.

We played with it for a while and I have to say, although it was a serious liability, we did have some fun. Graham was elected the chauffeur (there was no way that I was going to have driving lessons in a car like that) and, of course, he was happy as a pig in shit. We drove everywhere with the top down – even in sub-zero temperatures – and had the radio blasting at full volume at all times.

The first hint of real trouble came when a number 11 bus beat us away from the traffic lights at Clapham Common. That was when Graham first realised that there was something seriously wrong with the clutch. In retrospect, this is hardly surprising, as the car was seven or eight years old and Hilda drove like a stock car racer.

One day, I decided I should check if we had a spare tyre and on investigation I found the bottom of the boot (trunk to any Yanks reading this) full of rusty water. In a weak moment, I had lent the car to Graham to pick up and impress his latest girlfriend. Despite it being a freezing cold day, he insisted on taking the hood down, but the plastic rear window was not up to the shock and fractured. That is how all the rainwater found its way into the boot. Looking back, I must say it was almost worth the trouble it caused just to see Graham driving to meet his date in a woollen balaclava helmet that made him look like the poor man's Red Baron.

As if all of that wasn't bad enough, the windscreen wiper motor then packed up, and I had to ignominiously stand on the passenger seat and wipe the windscreen clear for Graham with a sponge and a handkerchief when it started to rain. I didn't want to offend my dear aunt, but this car was a liability that I just could not afford to live with any longer.

What has all this got to do with Jimmy Reed, you ask? Well, on one of our final sorties, we loaded up as many bodies as the car would take and drove south to the then-quaint country town of Guildford. There we witnessed Mr Reed perform at the previously mentioned Ricky Tick Club for a bunch of drunken farmers' sons.

Being devotees of the mush-mouthed maestro, we pulled a few strokes and managed to get backstage to meet our main man. I am afraid it was not an illuminating experience, for, true to his reputation, he sat slumped in a chair pissed out of his brain. It was a brief one-way conversation, as we couldn't understand a word he said.

You may be curious about what happened to the sporty Mercedes. My good buddy Cas Hitt found out that a garage owner in the nearby town of Cheam had a serious crush on such vehicles. The only part of the car in good order was the bodywork, so we set about accentuating this asset. We cleaned the white paintwork with Ajax bath cleaner, buffed it up with furniture polish and then ran it down hill in neutral to the garage forecourt in order to avoid the risk of slipping the clutch in front of the prospective purchaser. A deal was done and we drove away with an almost-new Mini and waved the white Mercedes goodbye. So there you have it. My brief flirtation with life's luxuries was over.

VI

Two streets east of Graham's flat in Hollywood Road was Redcliffe Road, where another blues enthusiast – coincidentally named Charles Radcliffe – lived with his girlfriend Diane. Charlie was a well-educated idealist. He spent much of his time writing about music – among other things – for a radical left-wing magazine with a fancy name that now escapes me. Diane worked at a recording studio, and during a casual conversation I found out that she had a friend who owned something I desperately wanted to get my hands on.

We would go around to the Radcliffe residence at weekends and just hang out and play music. The blues was a constant topic of conversation, and it so happened that John Lee Hooker's one-time partner, Eddie Kirkland, came into the conversation. I was keen to hear a hard-to-find album he had recorded for the Tru-Sound label in New York with the King Curtis band. Diane told me that she might be able to end my search, for she had a musician friend named Eric Clapton who actually owned a copy of the disc. She also confirmed that he was due to visit them the following weekend and she would ask him to bring it along.

Diane was true to her word. I called around the following Saturday morning just as Eric arrived with the album in a bag under his arm. He did not know me from Adam, but he did generously allow me to take the record away to record it. It was very trusting of him and I agreed to return the album the following week. Charlie matched his gesture by lending me a rare and treasured Woodrow Adams forty-five to record as well. That is when the trouble between us really began.

I took the records home and played them. The music was as good as I had anticipated, and I recorded both discs. The following week I returned to the Radcliffe flat and left the Kirkland album with Diane, telling her that Charlie's disc was inside the album sleeve for safekeeping. A week or two passed and I received an agitated phone call from Diane asking where was Charlie's treasured record. Apparently he couldn't find it, had gone ballistic, and I was to blame. I reminded her about putting it in Eric's album sleeve and she agreed to investigate the matter further. The record was not found, Charlie was inconsolable, and neither he nor Diane spoke to me ever again. So, Mr Clapton, if you did find that Woodrow Adams record, I hope you enjoyed it.

VII

Incredible as it must now seem, the established record companies were slow to catch on to the music that young people were interested in. As a result, new, smaller independent labels started to find operating space in the marketplace. One of these was fuelled by another character peripheral to our group.

Guy Stevens was a disc jockey at the Scene Club in Ham Yard just off Shaftsbury Avenue in London's West End. I became acquainted with him via the midday meet-ups at Dobell's Jazz Shop in the Charing Cross Road and at Lee's record stall at Cambridge Circus halfway up that same street.

Every time I bumped into Guy, he looked as if he had just woken up. In retrospect, I think this was a mistaken view, because I don't think he ever went to bed. He was certainly never a picture of good health at any time. He was so pale he would have needed Factor 50 sun cream for protection on the beach.

However, he had a fanatical enthusiasm for the music and a particular affection for danceable rhythm & blues. He somehow got hooked up with the already-established Island Records, who at that time were still aiming almost exclusively at the West Indian market. He started to lease some of our favourite r&b singles that were popular with the dancers at the Scene, issuing them on an Island subsidiary which he christened Sue after the New York label.

He would seldom be very concerned about the sound quality of his releases. If he could not get hold of the original masters, he would use his own records, or borrow ours in some cases, and just dub them with scratches and all. I can assure those of you who may have bought those Sue pressings that the vinyl discs were no different to those of other companies; it was the battered originals that the music was taken from that made some of them sound so awful.

One day, I met Guy walking south on the Charing Cross Road and he excitedly informed me that he was just about to issue an Elmore James album. I congratulated him and said that it would be a certain seller, for Elmore was hugely popular in underground blues circles. The conversation lasted a few minutes and I passed on by up the street. A few hundred yards further on I came to Lee's second hand record stall and there in a prominent box was a pile of Elmore James singles including the 1955 reissue of his rare first recording, 'Dust My Broom', on Ace Records. Clearly, Guy had achieved his aim and had just dispensed with the apparently superfluous source. Needless to say, I scooped up the items and purchased them for just a few shillings each. If anyone would now care to make me an offer for the Ace forty-five, be warned, a few shillings is not going to get it.

As for poor Guy, I am sure many of you will know that he got swept up in the rock'n'roll tidal wave. I believe he became the manager of the Clash or some other similar band and was washed-out and lifeless far too prematurely. Many r&b enthusiasts first heard the music due to his efforts and his compilations are now being nostalgically resurrected. He really deserved a better fate.

* * *

VIII

One of our earliest heroes was Bo Diddley. He didn't just have an exotic name, he also had a wonderful 'shave-and-a-haircut, two bits' jungle rhythm to go with it. Unlike his mainline blues contemporaries, he was more often regarded as a rock'n'roll artist. When he first visited these shores in 1963, it was as part of a rock'n'roll package show with the Everly Brothers as the main attraction. But guess who else was in the line-up, way down the running order? Yes, it was the new kids on the block, the Rolling Stones.

Graham and I thought that we ought to catch the tour, and decided upon a performance at the New Victoria Theatre in Central London. Before the show, we went for a drink in a pub across the way in Palace Street. We had been in touch with Brian, who joined us at the bar, and we were able to chat despite his face becoming increasingly well known to the public. Mind you, his appearance was becoming more conspicuous as his hair was now in an exaggerated 'pudding basin' style, and in those days anything out of the ordinary was immediately noticed.

He seemed relaxed and said he was enjoying the tour. He also informed us with great pride that the band had recorded 'Little Red Rooster' with the specific intention of trying to make the public more aware of the blues.

It was just a casual drink and I thought no more of it at the time. I just said, 'See you later,' and walked across the street to see the show. But it turned out there would be no more 'later', for that was the last time I ever saw him.

However, Graham did bump into him a few months afterwards while walking down Oxford Street. They started to chat in the usual way, but very soon they became encircled by a large crowd and had to agree to quickly end the conversation with a few parting words. They agreed to meet up again in the near future, but, of course, that never happened. Alas, Brian's name was soon added to the long list of the music business's premature casualties.

*   *   *

IX

Our small circle of blues enthusiasts included some colourful characters – none more so than Dave Godin. He was a very tall guy with bushy hair and wonderfully camp mannerisms. He lived in South-East London and was well acquainted with Mick, Keith and Brian. We would meet up with him regularly, for, prior to his deep affection for Motown and wrist-slashing tear-stained soul, he was a straight-ahead blues fan. Dave was a florist in those days and was always very amusing company. He worked at a shop near Charing Cross station, and I remember that at one of our parties he turned up with little flower arrangements for all the girls. There was one particularly memorable evening in his company that Anna and I always enjoy recalling.

One night a bunch of us were travelling together on the tube to a gig. We were discussing the impending arrival of Howlin' Wolf in Britain for a short tour. Dave had us in stitches as he held court. He was venting his concerns about how he should address the great man if he were fortunate enough to meet him. 'Well, what do I say if I meet him?' said Dave with an exaggerated lisp. 'What do I call him? Chester, Wolf, Howlin' or Mr Burnett?'

We were putty in his hands. The journey progressed and the subject matter changed. So, while no longer being the focus of attention, Dave and his friend pulled out balls of wool from a bag they were carrying and started knitting. We were all bemused except for Anna, who crossed to their side of the carriage and proceeded to advise them on complicated stitches. Yes, Dave was a great character and the r&b scene in Britain is indeed poorer for his passing.

X

In amongst all this hectic music activity, Anna and I got married in the March of 1965. It was a hastily-arranged event, at least partly motivated by the Income Tax rebate that would be forthcoming if we did the deed before the end of the current tax year. Anna made all the arrangements and I turned up on time. You could say we set a trend for some far more famous others to follow: a little while later, George Harrison got hitched at the same Epsom Registry Office. Anyway, we took the plunge on a Wednesday afternoon and Graham was my best man. This might not seem a very romantic event to some of you, but, nevertheless, we are still married to each other some forty years later. Many more lavish marriages have taken a quick fall at the first hurdle.

For as long as I can remember I have always had a burning desire to travel and see the world. Thankfully, Anna seemed to share my enthusiasm and was always happy enough to tag along. Unfortunately, back in those days there was no backpackers' infrastructure for young people to simply plug into. With very little competition between the airlines, travel was extremely expensive. The only way for me to take off was to try and get an advance contract of employment abroad. That would then secure tickets, a work permit and income.

Frankly, I would have gone anywhere as long as it was different. I had changed jobs yet again and was now working for an international civil engineering contactor based in South London. I had hoped they might have some overseas posting for me, but as none seemed in the pipeline, I took matters into my own hands. An advert in a technical journal caught my eye and I persuaded the office secretary to type an application for me. I soon found out that chance and fate can instantly and quite substantially change your life. I had applied for a job in Cyprus that I thought was a modest first step on my proposed world tour. However, the girl in the office got a digit wrong on the post office box number on the envelope.

To cut a very long story short, I received a reply and was invited for an interview in the bar at St Pancras railway station, which sounds like something out of a paperback detective novel. The guy I met had only returned to the country for a few days and was on his way to the North of England to visit relatives, hence the bizarre venue. Anyway he offered me a job in Uganda at twice the money I was currently earning.

Uganda! Where the hell was that? When Anna and I looked it up in the world atlas when I got home, we found it was in the centre of Africa. The redoubtable Anna agreed to come along for the ride, and three weeks later we were on a plane. We must have spent the better part of the next three years in Uganda, Kenya and Tanzania before moving on south. I am sure I could fill another book with all the things that happened to us *en route*, but there are some which are in keeping with the musical theme of this book.

Although I did take some vinyl albums with me, after a few months in the back of beyond I was getting serious music withdrawal symptoms. However, there was a small expatriate community in

Buddy Guy and his band of four other musicians drew big crowds since their Kenya tour started last Monday with a performance at Shanzu Teacher Training College in Mombasa, which was attended by the Mayor of Mombasa and the American Charge d'Affaires, Mr. Wendell Coote. Proceeds from two performances in Mombasa and Friday night's performance at the Nairobi City Hall went to the Kenya Association of Youth Centres. Last night's performance at Nairobi's Kaloleni Hall was in aid of the local charity Mji wa Huruma. Buddy, who is one of America's leading exponents of soul and blues music, and his band are on an eight-week tour of eight African countries, sponsored by the U.S. State Department. With Buddy in this picture is (left) Philip Guy.

Kampala and everyone knew everyone. Somehow, I ended up meeting the American cultural attaché from the US Embassy at one of the many parties in town. It sounds a very fancy title, but this was hardly Washington. I think his name was something like John Goodie, and he did everything except make the tea and clean the toilets. His claim to local fame was that he used to get funky forty-fives sent over to him from his mother, who I believe lived somewhere in the South. It was rumoured that they came in the diplomatic bag, and that made him very popular with the local partygoers – particularly me.

People were aware that I was a bit of a r&b fanatic, and one day he asked me if I knew of someone called Buddy Guy. 'Sure,' I replied, 'he's a Chicago blues singer,' and I told him that I had seen him

Phil Guy gets down at Kampala YMCA.

perform in London. Then he stopped me dead in my tracks by telling me that the American State Department had financed a cultural tour of independent African countries for Guy and his band, and that he was due in Uganda for a week of engagements. Here, in the middle of nowhere! I just couldn't believe it, but nevertheless it *was* true and it *did* happen.

When Guy and his band arrived, I was probably the only person in the whole of the country, black or white, to have ever heard of them before. Naturally, I used this to my advantage and managed to skilfully ingratiate myself and become their unofficial hanger-on. The guys in the band, which included Buddy's brother, Phil, and the great tenor sax player, A.C. Reed, were bemused by the whole tour, but they certainly had fun in Kampala. I don't think there was a mother in town whose daughter was safe for those seven days.

One amazing coincidence arose from that week, and I can tell you with certainty that it is a very small world we live in. For some thirty years later I literally bumped into the band's drummer, Charles Hicks, in a tiny nightclub on the West Side of Chicago. He was as surprised and shocked as I was to meet again, after such a long period, and on the other side of the globe. Even the band's roadie – then a young student named Jerry Ricks – visited Britain occasionally giving tutorials on acoustic guitar techniques.

Music was moving on pretty fast in the Western world while we were wandering around in Equatorial Africa. Most of my time was involved with helping build rural schools and hospitals, sometimes as far out as the Sudanese border. I did this along with World Bank-financed construction consultants from all parts of the world. One day, I ran across a couple of young American architects in Kampala who had just recently arrived in town. We were invited up to the house they were renting for an afternoon of drinking beer by the pool. Not an offer to be refused.

After sinking a few cold ones we got around to talking about music. One of them went into the house and came out with an album by some new band called Led Zeppelin. 'Have you heard this?' he asked. I shook my head and I turned the sleeve to find Jim's name as part of the group. Naturally I asked him to play it for me. The record hit the turntable and I can remember my reactions very clearly. There was the hiss of the stylus on first impact with vinyl, then BABABA-BOOM BOOM-BOOM! BABABA-BOOM-BOOM-BOOM! exploded from the speakers.

'Bloody hell! What was that?' was my instant response. I was just overwhelmed by the sound.

Hell, Jim, you really ***have*** *been working hard on your studio techniques, haven't you?* was my next reaction.

This was almost immediately followed by an outcry of 'You cheeky bastards!' as I realised I was listening to an old Muddy Waters song that we used to play back in Jim's front room, a number called 'You Need Love' from a four-track Pye EP with a picture of Muddy at Newport on the cover. Well, the four guys in this band had certainly taken it a 'whole lotta' somewhere else, and then some.

Years later, I was intrigued when a friend showed me a photograph of Jim playing a double-necked Gibson guitar. Even today it's an unusual instrument. However, it did amuse me to recall that the first person that Jim and I had ever seen with such an axe was the late, great Earl Hooker. Why did the memory raise a smile? Because Earl Hooker and his band were the musicians behind Muddy Waters on the infamous 'You Need Love'. But maybe that is just another of life's coincidences.

As I continued to listen to the album several other old blues themes were paraded in outlandish new clothes. There was even an extravagant instrumental track called ‘Moby Dick’, which was really little more than our old favourite, ‘Watch Your Step’ by Bobby Parker, only with the tempo slowed down and, of course, bags of other stuff piled on top. I pointed out these observations to the two architects, probably in my most sanctimonious ‘holier than thou’ manner. Understandably, they were not in the slightest bit interested, as this was all new and exciting music to them.

In retrospect, I can only think that their attitude was rather like our own view of the sedate acoustic blues of Sonny Terry & Brownie McGhee when we first discovered the tough electric blues of Chicago a few years before. As for poor old Bobby Parker, it took decades for him to get even the slightest bit of mass recognition. Even the Beatles used his memorable guitar figure as a template for ‘I Feel Fine’. Unfortunately, there are many sad stories like that. One thing was for sure: Heavy Metal had arrived and the blues was in for a bit of a battering for the next decade or so. However, the blues has a timeless resilience and the music resurfaced for the public to purr over again many years later.

XI

We are now nearing the end of the period I have tried to recall. I don’t really want to continue much further, for I would have to go over ground that is no doubt far more familiar to many of you. Others better qualified than myself have dealt with it many times before. However, I did think it would be worth considering how the music we loved so much has changed since those far off days.

When I started listening to the blues, one of the first fundamentals I learnt was the idea of the guitar being the ‘second voice’. Those who then analysed the music suggested that the accompanying instrument was like a companion offering moral support, rather like another voice saying ‘Right on!’ at the appropriate moment. Certainly the whole idea of a shared experience is something that I have witnessed and particularly enjoyed in black blues. I often lament the passing of those times, for the guitar is no longer the second voice. It has now become the first one and too often now has little or nothing new to say.

I am afraid I believe that the modern day obsession with the guitar has seriously eroded listeners' understanding and appreciation of the blues. Millions like the way the music sounds, but most don't really listen to the singers, or try to understand anything more about the subject matter. Songs that once conveyed so much have too often become short, meaningless vehicles for prolonged and increasingly frenzied guitar solos.

It took me many years to reach a point where I at least began to understand what the blues meant to the black audience it was originally intended for. The records that impressed and influenced us as young men were, of course, landmarks in our early knowledge-gathering. However, looking back on nearly fifty years of involvement with the music, I believe I learnt more about the essence of the blues from a relatively few live performances than countless hours listening to all those records. Certainly, some individual European club gigs stick in my memory, but I don't think I really started to appreciate the effect the music could have until I saw it performed in a black environment. It was a real eye-opener to find that the crowd knew every line of every song. Singers were supported by cries of encouragement or sympathy whenever the subject matter touched a raw nerve. Often, instrumental passages seemed to be there just to give the singer a break and I seldom, if ever, heard applause after a guitar solo. That habit seems to be for other folks in a different environment. Scholarly observation at a distance is all very well, but touch and feel is the way to get nearer to the heart and soul of the music.

Another lesson I learnt was that, in black society, women were the predominant supporters of the blues. Record companies who produced music for the black audience will tell you that the majority of their product was bought by, or for, women. This is all very different from the male guitar-hero worship that seems to exist now in the almost exclusively white marketplace. Watching the ladies in the house at a black blues gig is a real education. When one listens to the subject matter in the most popular blues songs it is then not hard to see the appeal to women, for most of the circumstances seem to revolve around them.

I can imagine you are now at the point of reaching for that 'purist' label to pin on me. Well, if you will allow me the chance, I will make a case suggesting that it is perhaps all those white rock/blues devotees who are the purists.

In my view, there has been a complete imbalance in the recent white generation's attitude to the blues. It seems to me that there has been an almost exclusive focus on a style of music and songs that was first performed more than fifty years ago. Some young musicians chose to try and faithfully replicate a bygone era, while others just took the music and dressed it up in heavy rock trappings. Whatever their motives, they did occasionally bring attention to the sources of their inspiration. This sometimes benefitted the artist and the listener, but sadly I believe there is a hidden tragedy associated with all the reverence that took place.

The Sixties saw the coming of the first white blues boom and the music flourished on almost all levels. However, fascination is often followed by a degree of disenchantment, and there was a distinct reaction in the Seventies. In the era of disco and concept albums, you couldn't find a blues gig to save your life. Time passed by, and the late Eighties and early Nineties saw a new generation discover the blues all over again. By then, most of the Fifties' giants were dead and the few who had survived, like John Lee Hooker, were treated as if they were royalty. The remaining dinosaurs were invited to resurrect their early successes to the accompaniment of a seemingly endless stream of older rock stars who suddenly discovered a mysterious new affection for the blues.

You might say that there is nothing wrong with all of that. Maybe better late than never? Unfortunately, while all this belated appreciation was going on, the new band of 'purists' ignored a whole generation of black blues artists who were alive and cooking on their doorstep south of the Mason-Dixon Line.

For one reason or another, in black music terms, the blues was dead on its feet back in the Seventies. Then in the early Eighties, right out of left field, a record came along that changed things dramatically – yet almost no one with blue eyes or blond hair took a blind bit of notice. That record was 'Down Home Blues', a simple but very effective song written by George Jackson and recorded by a then little-known journeyman named Z.Z. Hill.

The song touched a still-tender but neglected spot with black people all over America, not just in the South. Eventually it became a jukebox classic in every black club throughout the nation. Almost single-handedly, this song convinced a small group of Southern record companies that the blues was still a viable product, and for the next two decades a sadly neglected generation of modern blues singers kept the black record-buying public well satisfied with new and relevant songs.

While all this was going on, the new 'purists' continued looking over their shoulders at a bygone era. The majority of white listeners who actually heard contemporary blues during this period either regarded it as too soul-orientated to be blues, or not funky enough to be regarded as soul.

In the black community such differentials just didn't exist. For the everyday people who bought the records, these were just blues singers doing more or less what they had always done. Of course, the artists who wrote and performed the music didn't wear overalls and play harmonica or slide guitar. These were well-dressed singers who stood up to perform in front of equally smart bands with horn sections, synthesizers and sometimes backing singers. The songs that they sang were invariably related to all the familiar blues themes such as sex, betrayal, poverty and the like, but the lyrics were in modern-day language and terminology.

From the white perspective, most of the artists committed the unforgivable sin of not posturing with a guitar on the cover of their albums. How could they? Most of them don't play instruments – they leave that to others.

Regrettably, most of these singers have also now passed into history just like their predecessors, and I feel it very sad that they received so little recognition outside of their own community. Also, a great opportunity to enjoy their performances was missed, for here were living, working artists, not just legends with a faded photo on the reissue compilation sleeve. To learn that Mick Hucknall (of Simply Red) has now recorded an album of Bobby 'Blue' Bland material is not much consolation. Why does it always take so long to catch up?

Despite my frustration regarding these missed opportunities, the blues does still survive. In some ways, it has reverted to its origins and become a regional music again. In a handful of Southern states the Chitlin' Circuit is still active at the weekends, and a small number of independent companies continue to provide recorded music for mainly local consumption. Of course, it is not blues of the 'two guitars and a harmonica' variety. At the hole-in-the-wall clubs and outdoor BBQ gigs, the order of the day is contemporary, soul-drenched stuff that would probably have those 'purists' shaking their heads. But for me, and all those folks down there who know how to enjoy it…it's still the blues.

As an incidental observation, you might find it surprising, but I cannot readily recall the name of a black blues band. This is because the phrase 'blues band' is principally white terminology, and perhaps something that is particularly prevalent in Britain. In black blues circles it is the singer who is the attraction, and the bands are merely ensembles of musicians who provide the accompaniment. While on this subject I will take the opportunity to offer a little back-handed compliment to the Rolling Stones and to Led Zeppelin, for, unlike many others, they at least had the good judgement not to call themselves a blues band.

Right, that must have rattled a few rusty cages, so I think it's time to get down off my soap box. Perhaps this is where my tale should end. All of you know that Jim, Mick, Brian and Keith went on to big things and anything more that I could tell you about the subsequent months, years or decades has already been documented by countless others. Certainly Bill Wyman's amazingly detailed history, *Rolling With The Stones*, should be able to tell you everything you need to know about that band, and I am reliably informed that Jim is the habitual subject matter in countless guitar magazines.

Anyone who is interested in seeing the artists who actually took part in those *American Folk-Blues Festival* tours should seek out the four Hip-O DVDs that collect together the black & white TV film from that period. They are beautifully compiled presentations with very informative notes. I recently viewed the last two in the series and found it a rather unnerving experience. There for me to enjoy were solo performers such as Skip James, Bukka White and Son House, and I recalled how, as a young man, I sat in the audience and regarded them and their contemporaries as 'old blues guys'. It dawned on me that they were probably younger then than I am now – which is a very sobering thought that I choose not to dwell on.

Graham Ackers, Will Jones and I are now into the second half of our sixties. Our old habits die hard, and we continue to meet up for a few beers and still go to blues gigs, but I am afraid that the old brain cells are fading fast. So, as Graham suggests, if you want anything more, then we would need to go for hypnosis – and I think that is a step further than any of us want to take.

Yes, it was all a long time ago, and while it was enjoyable recalling those events, it was nowhere near as much fun as actually partaking in them.

INDEX

ILLUSTRATIONS & PHOTO CREDITS

Book cover on page 45 courtesy Bradt Travel Guides Ltd.

Label shot on page 60 courtesy author's collection; page 102 courtesy of Terry Kay.

Letters on pages 53, 61 and 62 courtesy author's collection.

Line drawing on page 45 copyright © Royston Ellis. Taken from *India by Rail* by Royston Ellis, first published in the UK by Bradt Travel Guides Ltd in 1989.

LP sleeves on pages 57, 63 and 72 courtesy author's collection.

Newspaper cutting on page 114 courtesy *Uganda Argus*/author's collection.

Photo on page 18 by and © David Williams; pages 29, 33, 66, 98, 99, 107 and 115 courtesy author's collection; page 38 by Don Stewart, courtesy of John Spicer/*Record Collector*; pages 84, 86, 87, 88, 90 and 91 by and © Brian Smith; page 76 courtesy Brian Smith collection; page 104 courtesy Music Mentor Books archive.

Programme on pages 75 and 80 courtesy author's collection.

OTHER TITLES FROM MUSIC MENTOR BOOKS

The A-Z of Buddy Holly and the Crickets
Alan Mann
ISBN-13: 978-0-9547068-0-7 *(pbk, 320 pages)*

The A-Z of Buddy Holly and the Crickets draws together a mass of Holly facts and info from a variety of published sources, as well as the author's own original research, and presents them in an easy-to-use encyclopaedic format. Now in its third edition, it has proved to be a popular and valuable reference work on this seminal rock'n'roller. It is a book that every Holly fan will want to keep at their fingertips. It is a book about a musical genius who will never be forgotten.

American Rock'n'Roll: The UK Tours 1956-72
Ian Wallis
ISBN-13: 978-0-9519888-6-2 *(pbk, 424 pages)*

The first-ever detailed overview of every visit to these shores by American (and Canadian!) rock'n'rollers. It's all here: over 400 pages of tour itineraries, support acts, show reports, TV appearances and other items of interest. Illustrated with dozens of original tour programmes, ads, ticket stubs and great live shots, many rare or previously unpublished.

Back On The Road Again
Dave Nicolson
ISBN-13: 978-0-9547068-2-1 *(pbk, 216 pages)*

A third book of interviews by Dave Nicolson in the popular *On The Road* series, this time with more of a Sixties flavour: Solomon Burke, Gene Chandler, Bruce Channel, Lowell Fulson, Jet Harris, Gene McDaniels, Scott McKenzie, Gary S. Paxton, Bobby 'Boris' Pickett, Martha Reeves & The Vandellas, Jimmie Rodgers, Gary Troxel (Fleetwoods), Leroy Van Dyke and Junior Walker.

The Chuck Berry International Directory (Volume 1)
Morten Reff
ISBN-13: 978-0-9547068-6-9 *(pbk, 486 pages)*

For the heavyweight Berry fan. Everything you ever wanted to know about Chuck Berry, in four enormous volumes compiled by the world-renowned Norwegian Berry collector and authority, Morten Reff. This volume contains discographies for over 40 countries, plus over 700 rare label and sleeve illustrations.

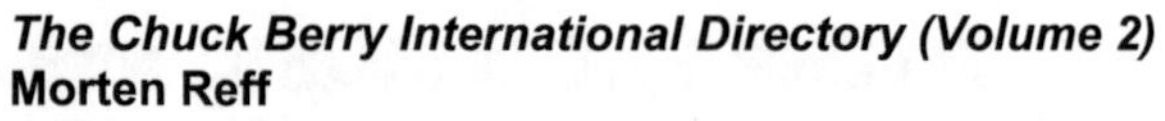

The Chuck Berry International Directory (Volume 2)
Morten Reff
ISBN-13: 978-0-9547068-7-6 ***(pbk, 532 pages)***

The second of four volumes in this extensive reference work dedicated to rock'n'roll's most influential guitarist and composer, Chuck Berry. Contains details of bootlegs; radio albums; movies; TV shows; video and DVD releases; international tour itineraries; hits, achievements and awards; Berry's songs, roots, and influence on other artists; tributes; Chuck Berry in print; fan clubs and websites; plus annotated discographies of pianist Johnnie Johnson (post-Berry) and the ultimate Berry copyist, Eddy Clearwater.

Daynce of the Peckerwoods: The Badlands of Texas Music
Michael H. Price
ISBN-13: 978-0-9547068-5-2 ***(pbk, 350 pages)***

From a childhood spent among such key roots-music figures as Bob Wills and Big Joe Turner, and an extended dual career as a musician and journalist, Michael H. Price has forged this frenzied chronicle of life among the denizens of the vanishing borderlands of Texas' indigenous music scene over the past half-century. Contains essays on Billy Briggs, Ornette Coleman, the Light Crust Doughboys, Big Bill Lister, Rudy Ray Moore, Eck Robertson, Ray Sharpe, Robert Shaw, Major Bill Smith, Stevie Ray Vaughan and many more.

Elvis & Buddy – Linked Lives
Alan Mann
ISBN-13: 978-0-9519888-5-5 ***(pbk, 160 pages)***

The achievements of Elvis Presley and Buddy Holly have been extensively documented, but until now little if anything has been known about the many ways in which their lives were interconnected. The author examines each artist's early years, comparing their backgrounds and influences, chronicling all their meetings and examining the many amazing parallels in their lives, careers and tragic deaths. Over 50 photos, including many rare/previously unpublished.

Last Swill and Testament
– The hilarious, unexpurgated memoirs of
Paul 'Sailor' Vernon
ISBN-13: 978-0-9547068-4-5 ***(pbk, 228 pages)***

Born in London shortly after the end of World War II, Paul 'Sailor' Vernon came into his own during the 1960s when spotty teenage herberts with bad haircuts began discovering The Blues. For the Sailor it became a lifelong obsession that led him into a whirlwind of activity as a rare record dealer, magazine proprietor/editor, video bootlegger and record company director. It's all here in this one-of-a-kind life history that will leave you reaching for an enamel bucket and a fresh bottle of disinfectant!

Let The Good Times Rock!
– A Fan's Notes On Post-War American Roots Music
Bill Millar
ISBN-13: 978-0-9519888-8-6 ***(pbk, 362 pages)***

For almost four decades, the name 'Bill Millar' has been synonymous with the very best in British music writing. This fabulous new book collects together 49 of his best pieces — some previously unpublished — in a thematic compilation covering hillbilly, rockabilly, R&B, rock'n'roll, doo-wop, swamp pop and soul. Includes essays on acappella, doo-wop and blue-eyed soul, as well as detailed profiles of some of the most fascinating and influential personalities of each era.

On The Road
Dave Nicolson
ISBN-13: 978-0-9519888-4-8 ***(pbk, 256 pages)***

Gary 'US' Bonds, Pat Boone, Freddy Cannon, Crickets Jerry Allison, Sonny Curtis and Joe B. Mauldin, Bo Diddley, Dion, Fats Domino, Duane Eddy, Frankie Ford, Charlie Gracie, Brian Hyland, Marv Johnson, Ben E. King, Brenda Lee, Little Eva, Chris Montez, Johnny Moore (Drifters), Gene Pitney, Johnny Preston, Tommy Roe, Del Shannon, Edwin Starr, Johnny Tillotson and Bobby Vee tell their own fascinating stories. Over 150 illustrations including vintage ads, record sleeves, label shots, sheet music covers, etc.

On The Road Again
Dave Nicolson
ISBN-13: 978-0-9519888-9-3 ***(pbk, 206 pages)***

In this second book of interviews with the stars of pop and rock'n'roll, Dave Nicolson delves deeper into the world of the music industry, with more revealing and highly personal first-hand accounts from 15 pioneering performers who were at the forefront of the Fifties' music revolution: Freddie Bell, Martin Denny, Johnny Farina (Santo & Johnny), the Kalin Twins, Robin Luke, Chas McDevitt, Phil Phillips, Marvin Rainwater, Herb Reed (Platters), Tommy Sands, Joe Terranova (Danny & The Juniors), Mitchell Torok, Marty Wilde and the 'Cool Ghoul' himself, John Zacherle.

Railroadin' Some: Railroads In The Early Blues
Max Haymes
ISBN-13: 978-0-9547068-3-8 ***(pbk, 390 pages)***

This groundbreaking book, written by one of the foremost blues historians in the UK, is based on over 30 years research, exploration and absolute passion for early blues music. It is the first ever comprehensive study of the enormous impact of the railroads on 19th and early 20th Century African American society and the many and varied references to this new phenomenon in early blues lyrics. Includes ballin' the jack, smokestack lightning, hot shots, the bottoms, chain gangs, barrelhouses, hobo jungles and more.

Music Mentor books are available from all good bookshops or by mail order from:

Music Mentor Books
69 Station Road
Upper Poppleton
YORK YO26 6PZ
England

Telephone: **+44 (0)1904 330308**
Email: **music.mentor@lineone.net**
Website: **http://musicmentor0.tripod.com**